THE LITTLE BOOK OF KNOWLEDGE:

HEAVY METAL

IDW

 Become our fan on Facebook **facebook.com/idwpublishing**
Follow us on Twitter **@idwpublishing**
 Subscribe to us on YouTube **youtube.com/idwpublishing**
See what's new on Tumblr **tumblr.idwpublishing.com**
Check us out on Instagram **instagram.com/idwpublishing**

ISBN: 978-1-68405-069-7   20 19 18 17   1 2 3 4

Ted Adams, CEO & Publisher
Greg Goldstein, President & COO
Robbie Robbins, EVP/Sr. Graphic Artist
Chris Ryall, Chief Creative Officer
David Hedgecock, Editor-in-Chief
Laurie Windrow, Senior Vice President of Sales & Marketing
Matthew Ruzicka, CPA, Chief Financial Officer
Lorelei Bunjes, VP of Digital Services
Jerry Bennington, VP of New Product Development

Created for Éditions Du Lombard by David Vandermeulen and
Nathalie Van Campenhoudt.
Original layout by Elhadi Yazi, Eric Laurin and Rebekah Paulovich.

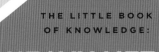

THE LITTLE BOOK
OF KNOWLEDGE:

HEAVY METAL

WRITTEN BY
JACQUES DE PIERPONT

ART BY
HERVÉ BOURHIS

TRANSLATION BY
EDWARD GAUVIN

EDITS BY
JUSTIN EISINGER AND ALONZO SIMON

COLLECTION DESIGN BY
RON ESTEVEZ

PUBLISHER:
TED ADAMS

FOREWORD

BY DAVID VANDERMEULEN

THE STORY OF A NAME

What a challenge it was to agree on a title for this book! Because if there's one thing Heavy Metal doesn't appreciate, it's being saddled with labels. Or rather, being reduced to a single denomination, since this incredible musical movement, which hasn't stopped evolving since the late '60s, has constantly created new niches: to date, it includes more than sixty-odd subgenres.

And so, no one would claim that any group Jacques de Pierpont covers in these pages actually belongs to the world of Hard Rock and not Heavy Metal. But is this really true? Have specialists in the field definitively settled such questions? Notorious *Rolling Stone* critic, gonzo journalist, and rock expert Lester Bangs[1] was far from the first to try and separate Hard Rock from Heavy Metal. According to Bangs, Hard Rock remained a musical trend spanning, quite precisely, 1968 to 1976, whereas Heavy Metal was primarily characterized by its themes (horror and science fiction) as well as the dress code of its fans (leather, badges, and studs).

In his *Dictionary of Rock*,[2] Michka Assayas suggests that Heavy Metal and Hard Rock can be seen as synonymous. Deep Purple and Judas Priest, in the same bag? Really? But Assayas' proposal isn't as ridiculous as it seems. If you ask me, Hard Rock specialist Jérôme Alberola has provided a firm, final answer to the question. He could not be clearer when he says: "The best definition of the difference between Hard Rock and Heavy Metal is, absurdly, the fact that there isn't one in any exact way.[3]"

But Alberola adds: "After just a few seconds of listening to a song, any true lover of the genre will immediately know which category to put it in, a distinction that will just as certainly escape the layperson. Classification is thus a matter of hearing and feeling, with the remarkable result that what should be a matter of the specific and subjective winds up an almost rational and obvious consensus among fans.[4]"

And so, while Lemmy Kilmister, emblematic bassist and singer for the group Motörhead, admired and respected by almost all of Heavy Metal fandom, has always stubbornly rejected the labels Hard Rock and Heavy Metal alike, claiming to be a musician of Rock 'n' Roll,[5] members of the group Accept continue to divide purists, bouncing between Rock and Metal from one album, and sometimes even one refrain, to the next. As we can see, it's hard to put a name to this untamable hydra, and even harder to write a nonfiction comic primer on the subject.[6]

A TRUE COMMUNITY

The first things newcomers to Metal will probably notice are the steadfast ties that unite the community, especially the peculiarly strong feeling of belonging that binds its members together. In fact, this unique characteristic can be observed throughout all Heavy

Metal. While in more traditional rock it's always been fashionable to reject or even disdain influence and heritage, the metal community has long stood out for its highly varied intergenerational connections. This was all the more striking when you saw how many kids flocking to the major summer festivals in 2015 were cheering for headliners as old as their grandparents: Black Sabbath (active since 1968), Alice Cooper (1969), Scorpions (1971), Judas Priest (1973), AC/DC (1974), Motörhead (1975), and even Iron Maiden[7] (1976)!

THE MOST ESTABLISHED COUNTERCULTURE

Another thing sure to strike readers of this book is the incredible vitality of the Metal movement. Over the decades, its range and variety seem to have flourished without interruption, now fanning out in vigorous exponential growth. Such that, with the exception of a few essential groups like those mentioned above, we might say that Heavy Metal has, for a good fifteen years now, been burdened by the unchecked growth of its own subgenres, depriving it of a primary through-line, a single undisputed leader. However, until one appears—or at least so long as the genre's dinosaurs still walk the earth—Heavy Metal's popularity seems in no way diminished by this scattering of its energies. Nor is this the biggest of Heavy Metal's many paradoxes: the bad reputation that has always dogged its fans remains an integral part of the genre. Fans revel in the bad rep that clings to Metal, right down to their combat boots—a rather skillfully maintained mark of pride. This is what prompted American sociologist Deena Weinstein to coin the expression "proud pariah"—proud pariahs, mocked, scorned or disdained; fans bound together by brotherly values, who have created a strong, marginal, and invisible culture.[8] Another sociologist, Frenchman Gérôme Guibert, highlights the paradox that in the U.S., Heavy Metal records are widely available in malls and concerts regularly fill stadiums, yet Metal always tops the list of answers to the question "What kind of music to you hate the most?" As ever, it remains a minority culture: ill-appreciated and most likely fated to stay that way.[9] Because as a culture, its codes and energies have always flown in the face of good taste. Probably also because Metal is a deeply proletarian movement, built on the dreams of countless children of the working-class the world over, who when faced with the adversity of their lot, found an identity in the sonic power and rich imagery of their musical heroes.

Though academia has for several years now been busy delving into such often disregarded topics as pornographic picture books and transsexuality, it was only in 2015 that Finland and England included Heavy Metal as a subject of study in their universities.

OUR CREATORS

A one-man institution in Belgium, Brussels native Jacques de Pierpont, a.k.a. Pompon, was one of the best-known hosts on francophone Belgian radio and television (RTBF), with no less than 40 years of daily shows about rock music, comics, science fiction, thrillers, punk, and above all, Heavy Metal![10] With his shows *Rock à Gogo* and *The Rockshow*, this great defender of overlooked music has without a doubt become one of the major Heavy Metal specialists now writing in French. Ronnie James Dio, Bruce Dickinson, Alice Cooper—he's interviewed them all.[11] As for highly eclectic music lover Hervé Bourhis, he was a natural choice for this book. He's already made himself a solid reputation as a discerning connoisseur of rock thanks to the success of his 45rpm album Rock and especially his comics collections *Le Petit livre Rock* [*The Little Book of Rock*] and *Le petit Livre Beatles* [*The Little Book of the Beatles*] from Éditions Dargaud.

NOTES

1. Bangs is irrevocably associated with *Rolling Stone*, despite only publishing a hundred or so articles in the magazine from 1969 to 1973, the year he was fired for disrespecting musicians. He died of his own excesses in 1982, at the age of 33.

2. Michka Assayas, *Dictionnaire du Rock* [*Dictionary of Rock*], Robert Laffont: Paris, 2002.

3. Jérôme Alberola, *Anthologie du Hard Rock : de bruit, de fureur et de larmes* [*Anthology of Hard Rock: Noise, Rage, and Tears*], Camion Blanc: Rosières-en-Haye, 2009.

4. *ibid.*

5. Something Lemmy had in common with the members of AC/DC.

6. We also considered simply calling this book "Metal," a word that some fans of Hard Rock and Heavy Metal can agree on, but we were afraid of leading metal and alloy enthusiasts astray.

7. In fact, the hearts and minds of generations of fans probably connected through Iron Maiden, especially with the rallying cry "Up the Irons!" which fans have been yelling for decades.

8. A certain metalhead fringe still proclaims the label "proud pariah" (the expression has since thrived), lamenting and rejecting Heavy Metal's media overexposure. See Deena Weinstein, *Heavy Metal: The Music and Its Culture*, rev. ed. Da Capo Press: Cambridge, 2000.

9. Interview with Gérôme Guibert in *Libération*, December 26, 2014.

10. The British had John Peel, the French had Bernard Lenoir, and the Belgians had Jacques de Pierpont. Our only regret is that RTBF never gave Pompon's shows much of a budget so he could offer the groups he played on air a chance to record live. More's the pity, since neither the Peel sessions (1967-2004) nor the Black Sessions (1992-2011) ever really gave Heavy Metal much of a spotlight. Proof once more that Metal is the red-headed stepchild of rock'n'roll.

11. Jacques de Pierpont retired from broadcasting in 2015. This book is a logical extension of his career, and his first work as an authority on rock and veteran of the front lines.

VADE RETRO SATANAS!

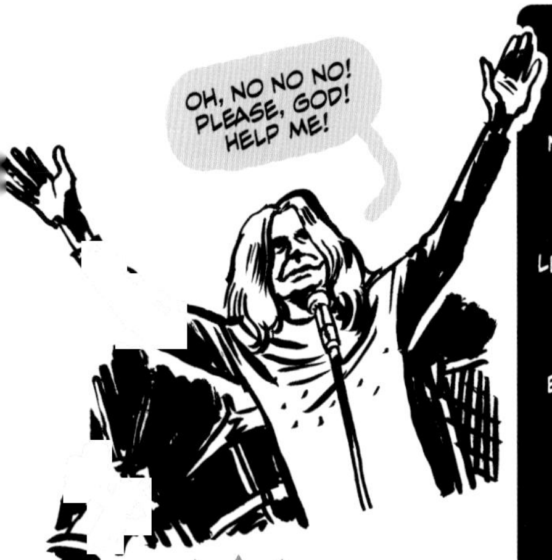

OH, NO NO NO! PLEASE, GOD! HELP ME!

← BLACK SABBATH

FEBRUARY, 1970: THIS ROCK GROUP FROM A WORKING CLASS BIRMINGHAM NEIGHBORHOOD HERALDS THE BIRTH OF METAL BY ENTREATING THE LORD...

THE SHORT-LIVED HIPPIE UTOPIA OF "PEACE & LOVE" IS NO MORE. JOHN LENNON SOUNDED ITS DEATH KNELL ("THE DREAM IS OVER" IN THE SONG "GOD").

HEAVY METAL WILL BE THE DISCORDANT AND TORMENTED EXPRESSION OF A TIME OF DISILLUSION. ALMOST HALF A CENTURY LATER, THIS FIENDISH OFFSPRING OF ROCK, SCORNED BY MUSIC CRITICS AND THE ESTABLISHMENT, HAS SPLIT INTO SEVERAL BRANCHES:

THRASH! DEATH! BLACK! ETC.

A FEW AJOR DATES

FESTIVALS ARE THE MAIN EVENTS OF THE "METAL COMMUNITY," THE MEETING PLACE OF ALL TRIBES (TOLERANCE IS THE RULE) AND GENERATIONS (RELATION IS PROUDLY PROCLAIMED)!

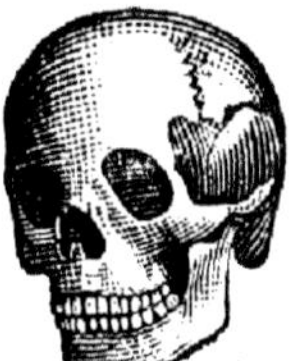

"THE CULTURE OF DEATH"

(to quote Christine Boutin, former French Minister) "is doing well, despite persistent heated opposition to Hellfest from sundry fundamentalist quarters..."

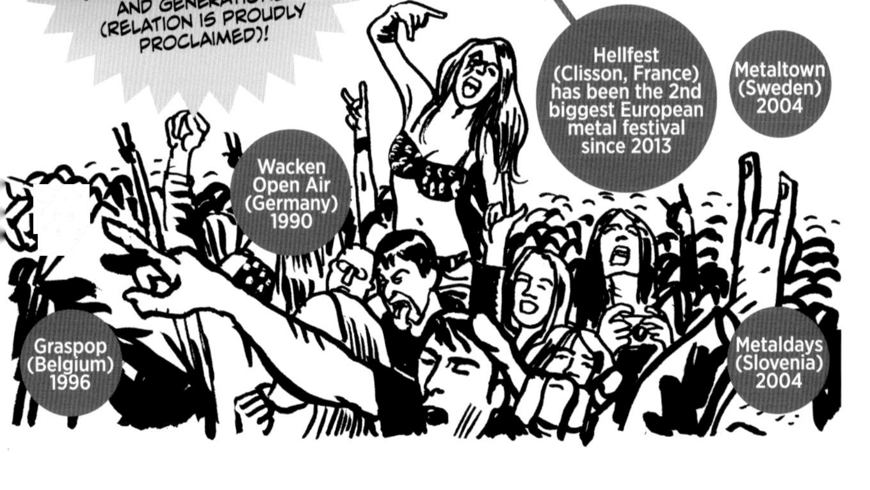

Hellfest (Clisson, France) has been the 2nd biggest European metal festival since 2013
Metaltown (Sweden) 2004
Wacken Open Air (Germany) 1990
Graspop (Belgium) 1996
Metaldays (Slovenia) 2004

HEAVYMETALSTYLE

A brief overview of classic outfits and dress codes on display at concerts...
or how fans make artists' style and poses their own.

THE BASICS (since the '80s)

LONG SMOOTH HAIR FOR "HEAD-BANGING"

LONG GOATEE, TATTOOS, AND PIERCINGS

STYLE BY SKATE FASHION AND HIP HOP

SLEEVELESS VEST WORN OVER BLACK LEATHER JACKET (A LEGACY OF BIKER CULTURE), ADORNED WITH BADGES, PATCHES, AND NUMBERS INDICATING AFFILIATION

CARTRIDGE BELT, CHAINS, AND STUDDED BRACELETS. BLACK DOMINATES.

BANDANAS (SHORT HAIR AND DREAD-LOCKS)

THE MODERNS (since the '90s)

CAMO FATIGUES, BAGGY OR CARGO SHORTS, AND HOODIES

METALHEADS LOVE FUN

POGO! SLAM!
MOSH PIT! ❶

STAGE DIVING! ❷

AIR GUITAR! ❸

HEAD BANGING! ❹

SIGN OF THE DEVIL!

A SIGN OF COMPLICITY BETWEEN ARTIST AND AUDIENCE, POPULARIZED IN 1980 BY SINGER RONNIE JAMES DIO (THEN HIGH PRIEST OF BLACK SABBATH).

IMMEDIATELY ADOPTED, SPREADING FROM CONCERT TO CONCERT LIKE WILDFIRE.

THE EVIL EYE

Tired of the classic peace sign, Dio remembered his Sicilian grandmother would make the "malocchio" gesture over her head when she lay down to sleep, to ward off the evil eye.

WEIRDNESS ➤

OF NOTE: THE SIGN OF THE HORNS COULD BE SPOTTED AS EARLY AS 1969, IN THE VISUALS OF COVEN, A PSEUDO-SATANIST GROUP WHOSE FIRST ALBUM, WITCHCRAFT DESTROYS MINDS & REAPS SOULS, ALSO FEATURED AN INVERTED CROSS AND A POSTER SHOWING THEIR NAKED LEAD SINGER OFFERED UP ON AN ALTAR TO THE DEMONS' APPETITES. THE FIRST TRACK WAS "BLACK SABBATH" BY BASSIST OZ OSBORNE (NOT TO BE CONFUSED WITH OZZY OSBOURNE FROM BLACK SABBATH, WHICH WOULD EMERGE ONE YEAR LATER).

THE ALMIGHTY RIFF!

IN THE MID-'60S, TECHNICAL INNOVATIONS LIKE BETTER DISTORTION CONTROL AND EQUIPMENT (MARSHALL STACKS, WAH WAH PEDALS) ALLOWED FOR HEAVIER, MORE AGGRESSIVE SOUNDS.

The Kinks 1964

"HARDER, FASTER, LOUDER"

CONCERTS TURNED INTO POWERFUL RITUALS. ALONG CAME THE "RIFF," A BRIEF MOTIF THAT SERVED AS THE SONG'S "HOOK."

THE BEGINNING OF A RACE TOWARD EXCESS WHOSE BASIC PRINCIPLES AC/DC WOULD SING:

LET THERE BE SOUND, AND THERE WAS SOUND
LET THERE BE LIGHT, AND THERE WAS LIGHT
LET THERE BE DRUMS, AND THERE WAS DRUMS
LET THERE BE GUITAR, AND THERE WAS GUITAR

LET THERE BE ROCK!

Deep Purple 1972

AC/DC 1979

POWER
Riffs consisted of "power chords," simplified combinations of two or three notes (the root note and the fifth, often with an octave doubling), with distortion compensating for the harmonic poverty.

BARRE
Power chords are played as barre chords on low strings and easily transposed: finger position doesn't change along the neck.

LARSEN
Once tamed, the famous Larsen effect went from being a nuisance to an asset: the saturated/compressed sound could be sustained/ modified in duration. A myriad of effects pedals exist today.

THE ROOTS OF EVIL

THE TERM **"HARD ROCK"** APPEARED IN GREAT BRITAIN IN 1968. IT WOULD PREVAIL IN EUROPE TILL THE LATE '80s, WHEREAS THE EXPRESSION **"HEAVY METAL"** TOOK HOLD IN THE USA.

A FEW PRECURSORS
SIXTIES

BLUE CHEER AND CREAM (A FORMAT KNOWN AS THE "POWER TRIO": BASS AND DRUMS CENTER STAGE), IRON BUTTERFLY (THE ALBUM *HEAVY* AND "IN-A-GADDA-DA-VIDA"), THE SONICS, MC5, AND THE STOOGES (WHO STOOD OUT WITH THEIR PUNK SAVAGERY ONSTAGE).

THE FIRST VIRTUOSOS OF DISTORTION

The Who ("My Generation"), Jimi Hendrix ("Purple Haze"), Jeff Beck and Jimmy Page (The Yardbirds), and even... The Beatles with their furious "Helter Skelter"!

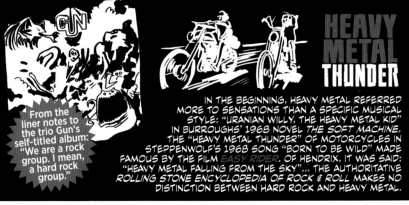

HEAVY METAL THUNDER

From the liner notes to the trio Gun's self-titled album: "We are a rock group. I mean, a hard rock group."

IN THE BEGINNING, HEAVY METAL REFERRED MORE TO SENSATIONS THAN A SPECIFIC MUSICAL STYLE: "URANIAN WILLY, THE HEAVY METAL KID" IN BURROUGHS' 1968 NOVEL *THE SOFT MACHINE*, THE "HEAVY METAL THUNDER" OF MOTORCYCLES IN STEPPENWOLF'S 1968 SONG "BORN TO BE WILD" MADE FAMOUS BY THE FILM *EASY RIDER*. OF HENDRIX, IT WAS SAID: "HEAVY METAL FALLING FROM THE SKY"... THE AUTHORITATIVE *ROLLING STONE ENCYCLOPEDIA OF ROCK & ROLL* MAKES NO DISTINCTION BETWEEN HARD ROCK AND HEAVY METAL.

LED ZEPPELIN

JIMMY PAGE (GUITAR), ROBERT PLANT (VOCALS), JOHN BONHAM (DRUMS), AND JOHN PAUL JONES (BASS): THE PERFECT ENSEMBLE OF SYNCRETIC INVENTIVENESS AND RHYTHMIC POWER.

ESOTERIC!!

THE COVER OF THE GROUP'S MYTHIC FOURTH ALBUM IN 1971 MAKES NO MENTION OF THE GROUP'S NAME, ADORNED INSTEAD WITH DRUIDIC RUNES MEANT TO REPRESENT EACH OF ITS MEMBERS. KEEN ON THE OCCULT, JIMMY PAGE LIVED IN THE FORMER MANOR OF THE MAGE ALEISTER CROWLEY.

CONTROVERSY

UNLIKE CLAPTON, WHO REVERENTLY CITED HIS SOURCES, PAGE AND PLANT DID NOT FLAG THEIR FLAGRANT BORROWINGS: THE THEME TO "WHOLE LOTTA LOVE" CAME FROM WILLIE DIXON'S "YOU NEED LOVE," THOUGH IT WAS HEAVILY "ZEPPELINIZED."

THE MOST FAMOUS

After a blues-heavy start (1969) came a fascinating mixture of furious explosion ("Rock and Roll", "Black Dog") and sophisticated compositions ("Stairway to Heaven", "Kashmir") that ranged from proto-Heavy Metal ("Communication Breakdown") to folk ("Gallows Pole") over the course of heavily worked-over albums

THE HARD ROCK PANTHEON: THE BRITISH TRINITY
DEEP PURPLE

AT FIRST, THE GROUP WAS TEMPTED BY PROGRESSIVE ROCK AND A CONNECTION WITH CLASSICAL MUSIC. BUT IN THEIR BEST-KNOWN INCARNATION (IAN GILLAN ON VOCALS, RITCHIE BLACKMORE ON GUITAR, ROGER GLOVER ON BASS, JON LORD ON THE ORGAN, IAN PAICE ON DRUMS), IT TOOK A RADICAL TURN WITH THE ALBUMS *IN ROCK* (1970), AND *MACHINE HEAD* (1972). THE GROUP LAUNCHED THE VOGUE FOR LIVE ALBUMS (*MADE IN JAPAN*).

DESCENDANTS

RITCHIE BLACKMORE FOUNDED RAINBOW IN 1975 WITH SINGER RONNIE JAMES DIO, LATER OF BLACK SABBATH (ALBUM: *RISING*, 1976). WHITESNAKE IN 1978 WITH DAVID COVERDALE (WHO SUCCEEDED IAN GILLAN IN DEEP PURPLE IN 1973, ALONG WITH JON LORD AND IAN PAICE). IN 1991, A GROOVE THRASH METAL GROUP NAMED MACHINE HEAD WAS FORMED IN CALIFORNIA.

Whitesnake

THE MOST HIGHBROW

Their style: rock that was spirited ("Speed King") and epic ("Child in Time"), high-pitched singing coupled with solos criss-crossing between keyboard and guitar, influenced by 17th-century baroque music ("Highway Star").

The group was influenced by Bach on their 1969 album, *Concerto for Group and Orchestra*.

THE HARD ROCK PANTHEON: THE BRITISH TRINITY
BLACK SABBATH

CARRIED BY OZZY OSBOURNE'S MONOTONOUS VOICE, TONY IOMMI'S HYPNOTIC RIFFS AND THE HEAVY RHYTHMS OF DRUMMER BILL WARD, BASSIST GEEZER BUTLER'S LYRICS EXPRESSED CONFUSED BUT DEEP-SEATED DISTRESS. HE'D BEEN TRAUMATIZED BY A CATHOLIC EDUCATION THAT MADE HIM FEAR SATAN MORE THAN HE LOVED GOD...

TI E DARKEST

Their songs, studded with references to the Lovecraftian Weird ("Behind the Wall of Sleep"), Tolkien ("The Wizard"), and science fiction ("Into the Void"), sketched an apocalyptic vision of the world between fear of the demon ("N.I.B." – Nativity in Black) and dreams of redemption ("After Forever"). Alienation ("Iron Man"), fear of loneliness ("Paranoid") and madness ("Wheels of Confusion"), apologia followed by rejection of hard drugs ("Snowblind" vs. "Hand of Doom"), odes to cannabis ("Sweet Leaf"), dread of nuclear conflict ("Electric Funeral"), rebellion ("War Pigs"), hope of peace at last ("Children of the Grave")... Sabbath was a long way from the insouciant hedonism of its peers.

BLACK SABBATH

AGAINST THE TIDES OF VIRTUOSO SPEED, BLACK SABBATH ESTABLISHED A SLOW, HEAVY, TORMENTED STYLE THAT WOULD BECOME ITS OWN SCHOOL.

THE WEIRD

THE BAND TOOK ITS NAME FROM AN ITALIAN HORROR MOVIE BY MARIO BAVA, HOSTED BY BORIS KARLOFF.

BLOODY SABBATH

Their first two albums, released in 1970

THE LIMITS OF ITS MUSICIANS ALSO CONTRIBUTED TO SABBATH'S APPEAL. OSBOURNE, HIS TONE BY TURNS MENACING AND MOURNFUL, COULD ONLY STAY IN TUNE BY CLOSELY FOLLOWING THE INSTRUMENTAL MELODY. IN HINDSIGHT, BLACK SABBATH SEEMS *THE TRUE ORIGINATOR OF HEAVY METAL*, THE DIRECT SOURCE OF MANY OF ITS LATER TRENDS: THRASH, BLACK, DOOM... FROM JUDAS PRIEST TO METALLICA, IRON MAIDEN TO KYUSS, MOST METAL MUSICIANS WOULD POINT TO IT AS THEIR PRIMARY INSPIRATION ON ALL LEVELS (STYLE, THEME, IMAGERY).

ESSENTIAL ALBUMS: *BLACK SABBATH* AND *PARANOID* (1970), *MASTER OF REALITY* (1971), *SABBATH BLOODY SABBATH* (1973), AND FINALLY, *SABOTAGE* (1975).

SAPOTAGE!

Iommi lost the tips of two fingers on his right hand in an accident while working in a sheet metal factory. In order to play without pain, he slackened his guitar strings to lower pitches—from E to C#—a tuning that made for a heavier sound.

DIABOLUS IN MUSICA

TONY IOMMI MADE USE OF TRITONES, BUT WHAT ARE THEY? SO NAMED DURING THE MIDDLE AGES, WHEN THEY WERE BANNED, TRITONES ARE DISSONANT INTERVALS THAT WERE CONSIDERED SHOCKING TO CHRISTIAN EARS. AS A RESULT, HEAVY METAL USED THEM JOYOUSLY. FOR INSTANCE: THE THREE TONES BETWEEN THE NOTES G AND C# (RIFF FOR THE SONG "BLACK SABBATH"). TRITONES WERE LATER REDEEMED IN BAROQUE MUSIC.

HARD ROCK SEVENTIES

THE USA

Aerosmith, Blue Öyster Cult, Cactus, Grand Funk Railroad, Mountain, Ted Nugent, ZZ Top... and more mainstream or "radio-friendly": Boston, Journey, Foreigner ("Hard FM")

IN GREAT BRITAIN

FREE, HAWKWIND, HUMBLE PIE, JETHRO TULL, KING CRIMSON, NAZARETH, SLADE, SPOOKY TOOTH, MOTT THE HOOPLE, THIN LIZZY, UFO, URIAH HEEP, QUEEN...

MAY BLITZ

IN CONTINENTAL EUROPE

GOLDEN EARRING, KROKUS, SCORPIONS

SCORPIONS

...AND A FEW NEGLECTED GROUPS WORTH RESCUING

Captain Beyond, May Blitz, Lucifer's Friend, Bloodrock, Buffalo

TOWARD HEAVY METAL: 10 YEARS OF GESTATION
ALICE COOPER

DISCOVERED BY FRANK ZAPPA, VINCENT FURNIER'S GROUP (HE WAS THE SON OF A PREACHER—NOT A RARITY IN THE HISTORY OF ROCK) GOT NOTICED FOR ITS 1972 ALBUM *SCHOOL'S OUT*. HIS KEEN SENSE OF IRONIC EXCESS, DRAWN FROM HORROR MOVIES AND GRAND GUIGNOL THEATRE, CAUSED A SCANDAL.

SHADOWS

FURNIER SHOWED UP IN MOVIES AND ON TV: JOHN CARPENTER'S *PRINCE OF SHADOWS*, AND RACHEL TALALAY'S *FREDDY'S DEAD*... AND *THE MUPPET SHOW*!

THE MAGICIAN AND SINGER PURSUED A SOLO CAREER UNDER THE SAME NAME (*WELCOME TO MY NIGHTMARE*, 1975), WITH VARIED SUCCESS.

GRAND GUIGNOL?

Special effects by the bucketful (dismembered dolls full of fake blood, snakes and spiders) and macabre sets (gallows, electric chair, guillotine: Alice went so far as to fake his suicide in concert).

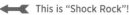 This is "Shock Rock"!

SHOCK ROCK!

PIONEERS OF THE GENRE: SCREAMIN' JAY HAWKINS (HE CAME ONSTAGE IN A COFFIN, DRESSED AS A VAMPIRE, IN 1956) AND THE CRAZY WORLD OF ARTHUR BROWN (WITH HIS CROWN OF FLAMES - FIRE, 1968).

TOWARD HEAVY METAL: 10 YEARS OF GESTATION
KISS

OPPORTUNISTIC AND
UNSCRUPULOUS, KISS IS A
CARICATURE, THE AMERICAN
HEIR TO ANDROGYNOUS BRITISH
GLAM ROCK (BOWIE, T-REX).
TEENS FLOCKED TO THEIR
CONCERTS THE WAY THEIR
(SCANDALIZED) PARENTS
HAD ONCE FLOCKED TO THE
CIRCUS. HORRIFIC BLACK-
AND-WHITE MAKEUP,
SEQUINED BURLESQUE
COSTUMES, PLATFORM
HEELS, CUSTOM ROCKET-
SHAPED GUITARS, THE
KISS FOURSOME PLAYED
AT BEING CARDBOARD
SUPERHEROES.

KISSMANIA

AN IMPRESSIVE
INTERNATIONAL
FAN CLUB, THE
KISS ARMY,
GREEDILY
LAPPED UP
AN ARRAY
OF LICENSED
PRODUCTS THAT
COUNTED FOR
AS MUCH AS THE
ACTUAL ALBUMS
AND PYROTECHNIC CONCERTS: ACTION
FIGURES, MAKEUP KITS... EVEN A
PINBALL GAME! BUSINESS
WAS BOOMING!

KISS:
heroes of a
1977 Marvel
comic!

CARNIVAL!

Their bubble gum hard rock drifted
all the way over into disco (the 1979 hit
"I Was Made for Lovin' You"). Their brief
experiment with not wearing makeup
in the '80s was doomed to failure.

TOWARD HEAVY METAL: 10 YEARS OF GESTATION
AC/DC

THE AUSTRALIAN ARCHETYPE OF MUSCLE ROCK, MISCHIEVOUS AND LEWD. LED BY THE YOUNG BROTHERS (ANGUS THE IMPISH SOLOIST ON GUITAR, AND MALCOLM THE UNDERSTATED MAINSTAY ON BASS) AND BON SCOTT THE JOKESTER (VOCALS), ALTERNATING CURRENT/DIRECT CURRENT (IN OTHER WORDS: SWINGS BOTH WAYS) PILED ON STORIES OF HELLISH TOURS ("IT'S A LONG WAY TO THE TOP (IF YOU WANNA ROCK'N'ROLL)") WITH RAUNCHY PIT STOPS.

BLACK IS BLACK

THEIR RISE WAS RAPID BUT SMALL-SCALE. THIS WAS AN ERA OF CLUBS WHERE BON SCOTT WOULD VENTURE INTO THE CROWD FOLLOWED BY ANGUS, GUITAR ON HIS BACK, AND PLACE A CALL TO AN AS-YET UNKNOWN FRENCH GROUP (TRUST), ASKING THEM IF THEY WANTED TO OPEN FOR AC/DC IN PARIS.

YOUNG AND INNOCENT

From *High Voltage* (1975) to *Highway to Hell* (1979), their journey was flawless. Back in their native Scotland in 1978, before a white-hot audience, right before the song "The Jack," they asked: "Any virgins in Glasgow?"
—cf. the live album *If You Want Blood*.

IF YOU WANT BLOOD ...

TOWARD HEAVY METAL: 10 YEARS OF GESTATION

JUDAS PRIEST

FORMED AS A KEYBOARDLESS, TWO-GUITAR QUINTET (GLENN TIPTON AND K.K. DOWNING, SWITCHING OFF ON GUITAR AND BASS). SHORT, STACCATO MELODIC FIGURES, ROB HALFORD'S PIERCING VOCAL RANGE. AN ARRAY OF S&M IMAGERY (LEATHER, STUDS, WHIPS, AND CIRCUSLIKE SETS). IT WAS HARD TO DO BETTER (OR WORSE) THAN HAVING YOUR LEAD SINGER MAKE HIS ENTRANCE ON A HARLEY DAVIDSON.

IN CONCERT, JUDAS PRIEST'S INFLUENCE WAS IMMENSE. OTHER GROUPS WOULD ADOPT ALMOST ALL THE SONGS FROM THE LIVE ALBUM UNLEASHED IN THE EAST (1979) AS THEIR NAMES: EXCITER, SINNER, TYRANT...

BRITISH STEEL

Black Sabbath had laid the foundations for heavy metal. Now it was up to Judas Priest (also from the Birmingham area, and initially tempted by a more glam style) to begin building with the albums *Stained Class*, *Killing Machine* (1978), and especially *British Steel* with the hymns "Living After Midnight" and "Breaking the Law" (1980).

Despite close ties to the gay scene, Rob Halford would wait until 1998 before daring to come out of the closet.

The group's name comes from Bob Dylan's song "The Ballad of Frankie Lee and Judas Priest."

TOWARD HEAVY METAL: 10 YEARS OF GESTATION
HARDER, FASTER, LOUDER PT. 2

THE TRAJECTORY OF JUDAS PRIEST (BUT ALSO THAT OF SCORPIONS IN GERMANY, STARTING WITH THE ALBUM *BLACKOUT* IN '82) REFLECTS...

THE SLIPPAGE OF HARD ROCK TOWARD HEAVY METAL

...THAT BEGAN IN THE MID-'70S: NO MORE REFERENCES TO THE "BLUES," TIGHT COMPOSITIONS THAT LEFT LITTLE ROOM FOR IMPROVISATION, AND A PENCHANT FOR DISPLAYS OF VIRTUOSITY, OF WHICH GUITARIST EDDIE VAN HALEN WAS THE FIRST PARAGON.

VAN HALEN

On Van Halen's first album (1978), between two strong riff machines ("Runnin' with the Devil" and "You Really Got Me"), the instrumental "Eruption"—a solo by Eddie—reeled off a substantial display of technical expertise in just three minutes.

Eddie Van Halen using his "tapping" technique

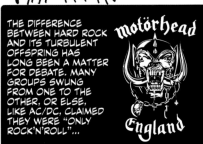

THE DIFFERENCE BETWEEN HARD ROCK AND ITS TURBULENT OFFSPRING HAS LONG BEEN A MATTER FOR DEBATE. MANY GROUPS SWUNG FROM ONE TO THE OTHER, OR ELSE, LIKE AC/DC, CLAIMED THEY WERE "ONLY ROCK'N'ROLL"...

MOTÖRHEAD

GROUP FOUNDED IN 1975 BY LEMMY KILMISTER (BORN 1945, BASSIST FOR THE PSYCHEDELIC BAND HAWKWIND FROM '71-'75). A FAN OF OLD-TIME ROCK'N'ROLL (BUDDY HOLLY) AND CLOSE IN SPIRIT TO PUNK REBELS, ALL DISCIPLES OF "HEAVY ROCK" OF ALL GENERATIONS WORSHIPPED LEMMY: FOR STAYING FAITHFUL TO THE VERY PERSONAL STYLE HE'D FORGED (DOUBLE STOPS AND CHORDS ON HIS RICKENBACKER BASS), FOR HIS INDIFFERENCE TO CONVENTIONAL STANDARDS OF BEAUTY (HE WAS PROUD OF HIS WEATHERBEATEN FACE), FOR HIS IMMUTABLY AUSTERE LOOK (ALL IN BLACK, FROM HIS COWBOY HAT TO HIS BOOTS, BANDOLIER, IRON CROSS, AND ACE OF SPADES).

SPEED FREAK

THAT'S WHAT THE WORD "MOTORHEAD" MEANS IN SLANG.

His sheer physical endurance (despite excessive amounts of amphetamines and bourbon) is a medical mystery, but he resolved to slow down in 2014.

NO SLEEP

The self-proclaimed loudest group the world (a title disputed by Manowa *Everything Louder Than Everyor Else,* was a '99 live albu

INFLUENCES

MOTÖRHEAD WAS A CONSIDERABLE INFLUENCE ON THRASH METAL. METALLICA WOULD PAY HIM A HANDSOME TRIBUTE IN 1995 (DRESSED AS LEMMY, THE MEMBERS OF METALLICA JOINED HIM ONSTAGE FOR A MINI-CONCERT IN HOMAGE). YOUNG LARS ULRICH, THE GROUP'S FUTURE DRUMMER, WAS THE PRESIDENT OF MOTÖRHEAD'S U.S. FAN CLUB.

Deaf as a post, Lemmy was a nightmare for sound techs.

THE EIGHTIES: THE TRIUMPH OF HEAVY METAL

1980: A PIVOTAL YEAR

THE DEMISES OF BON SCOTT AND DRUMMER JOHN BONHAM, VICTIMS OF THEIR OWN EXCESS AND BENDERS, SEEMED THE DEATH KNELL OF AN ERA. IF BONHAM'S PASSING MARKED THE END OF LED ZEPPELIN, AC/DC DECIDED TO GO ON (MALCOLM YOUNG: "I'M NOT GONNA SIT AROUND MOPIN' ALL FUCKIN' YEAR.") WITH SINGER BRIAN JOHNSON.

THE ALBUM BACK IN BLACK WAS BOTH A REQUIEM ("HELLS BELLS" SOUNDED THE ALARM) AND A DECLARATION OF FAITH ("BACK IN BLACK": "WELL I'M BACK/YES I'M BACK"). IT MET WITH ENORMOUS SUCCESS: AC/DC PACKED STADIUMS WITH GIANT SETS (A ONE-TON BELL AND, LATER, CANNONS AND GIANT INFLATABLE DOLLS).

AC/DC

BACK IN BLACK

NEW LIFE

Black Sabbath also began a new life, without Ozzy Osbourne in '78, bouncing back with ex-Rainbow Ronnie James Dio and lyrical charisma (the albums *Heaven and Hell* in '80 and *Mob Rules* in '81). Dio went solo (*Holy Diver* in '83), and later teamed up with Iommi and Butler as the group Heaven and Hell in 2006. He died in 2010, at the age of 67.

BLACK SABBATH

HEAVEN AND HELL

Osbourne moved to California, where his future wife, Sharon—the daughter of Sabbath's manager—took his career in hand and saved him from decline. Supported by a fine guitarist and composer,

RANDY RHOADS,

Ozzy made a confident return with the albums *Blizzard of Ozz* and *Diary of a Madman.* His most significant successor would be Zakk Wylde.

Rhoads died in 1982 in a plane crash.

OZZY

OSBOURNE WOULD BE BOTH GODFATHER TO A NEW GENERATION OF GROUPS (THE FESTIVAL TOUR OZZFEST, STARTING IN 1996) AND A CLOWNISH ECHO OF HIS FORMER SELF WITH HIS FAMILY IN MTV'S REALITY SHOW *THE OSBOURNES* FROM 2002-05.

THE EIGHTIES: THE TRIUMPH OF HEAVY METAL
MONSTERS OF ROCK

IN ENGLAND, WHILE
MONSTERS OF ROCK,
THE FIRST-EVER ALL-METAL
FESTIVAL, DREW 60,000
FANS TO DONINGTON ON
AUGUST 16 (JUDAS PRIEST,
RAINBOW, SCORPIONS),
WHAT WAS SOON DUBBED
THE "NEW WAVE OF
BRITISH HEAVY METAL"
(NWOBHM) AROSE,
COMBINING THE DIY
PHILOSOPHY OF PUNK
ROCK (FANZINES, CLUBS,
AND INDIE LABELS) WITH
METAL'S POWERHOUSE
SOUND.

NWOBHM

IN THE WAKE OF JUDAS PRIEST AND
MOTÖRHEAD, DOZENS OF GROUPS
WERE FORMED. AMONG THE MOST
POPULAR: DIAMOND HEAD (METALLICA
ADMIRED THEIR ALBUM *LIGHTNING
TO THE NATIONS*), SAXON (ALBUMS:
WHEELS OF STEEL AND *POWER AND
THE GLORY*. THEIR LIVE
ALBUM *THE EAGLE
HAS LANDED*
GAVE A GOOD
SENSE OF
THE FESTIVE
ATMOSPHERE
AT
CONCERTS).

LIGHTNING TO THE NATIONS

SOUNDS HEAVY METAL SPECIAL

No.1 June 1981 50p

KERRANG!

featuring
the
official
All-Time
HM
Top
100!

In colour . . .
MOTÖRHEAD!
GIRLSCHOOL!
UFO! SAXON!
KISS! TRUST!
SCHENKER!
WILD HORSES!
PAT BENATAR! Z Z TOP!
STYX! VARDIS! TED NUGENT!
BLACKFOOT! GRAHAM BONNET!
RONNIE MONTROSE! ROSE TATTOO!

Backed
by *Kerrang!* the
metal supplement
to the weekly mag
Sounds. It had
a massive
impact.

Kerrang! becam
its own magazine i
1981. Other veteran
of the metal pres
Aardschok (Th
Netherlands, 198(
and *Rock Har*
(Germany, 1983

DEF LEPPARD (*PYROMANIA* IN '83
AND *HYSTERIA* IN '87) WAS A HIT IN
THE USA. AFTER A CAR ACCIDENT IN
WHICH HE LOST HIS LEFT ARM, THE
DRUMMER HAD A CUSTOM KIT MADE
SO HE COULD KEEP PLAYING.

THE EIGHTIES: THE TRIUMPH OF HEAVY METAL
IRON MAIDEN

IRON MAIDEN BECAME THE SPEARHEAD OF THE NWOBHM MOVEMENT WITH "RUNNING FREE," SOON FOLLOWED BY THE ALBUM *KILLERS*. HEADED BY BASSIST-COMPOSER STEVE HARRIS, MAIDEN STOOD OUT FOR THE QUALITY OF ITS SONG-WRITING (SOPHISTICATED MELODIC LINES, FEVERISH JOUSTING BETWEEN GUITARISTS, EPIC SINGING) AND HIGHLY PLAYFUL MACABRE IMAGERY. THE FIGURE OF EDDIE, A ZOMBIE-LIKE PUNK, SOON BECAME THEIR PERENNIAL MASCOT ONSTAGE, WITH HIS SARDONIC RICTUS AND BLOOD-SOAKED MISDEEDS.

KILLERS

MAIDEN EXPLODED ONTO THE SCENE IN 1982 WITH THE ALBUM *THE NUMBER OF THE BEAST*. SINGER PAUL DI'ANNO WAS REPLACED BY BRUCE DICKINSON, FORMERLY OF SAMSON, A FENCING ENTHUSIAST WHO COULD TRANSFORM THE STAGE INTO A THEATRICAL, ATHLETIC OBSTACLE COURSE WITHOUT SACRIFICING ANY VOCAL POWER. DI'ANNO HAD BEEN PERFECT IN SMALLER CLUBS, BUT NOW HARRIS SAW HIM AS A HINDRANCE TO THE GROUP'S NEW AMBITIONS.

Illustrator Derek Riggs is the group's sixth member!

Coincidence:
Iron Maiden, founded in 1976, also became the nickname of Margaret Thatcher, who came to power in May 1979. Work was cut out for Eddie, who loved his country but not its leader.

THE EIGHTIES: THE TRIUMPH OF HEAVY METAL

TRUST

IN FRANCE, CARRIED BY THE POWERFUL BERNIE BONVOISIN (VOCALS) AND NONO (GUITAR), TRUST SPAT OUT ITS WRATH IN STRONG, REBELLIOUS SONGS ("L'ÉLITE"). TIES WITH BON SCOTT RESULTED IN OPENING FOR AC/DC AT A CONCERT AT THE STADIUM DE PARIS ON OCTOBER 24, 1978. WHEN THEY RECORDED THEIR FIRST 45, "PARIS BY NIGHT" (INSPIRED BY THE AC/DC SONG "LOVE AT FIRST FEEL"), BONVOISIN WOULD PAY TRIBUTE TO BON SCOTT IN '81 IN THE MOVING SONG "YOUR FIRST ACT."

BEHIND TRUST

OTHER GROUPS TRIED THEIR CHANCES, IN FRENCH AND/OR ENGLISH—ATTENTAT ROCK, DEMON EYES, H-BOMB, MASSACRA, SATAN JOKERS, SORTILÈGE, VULCAIN, WARNING—WITHOUT ANY REALLY MANAGING TO BREAK THROUGH, FOR LACK OF MEDIA SUPPORT AND EFFECTIVE BACKING. SOME, LIKE ADX, KILLERS, AND LOUDBLAST (THE BEST-KNOWN, *SUBLIME DEMENTIA*, '93) ARE STILL AROUND TODAY.

REPRESSION

Trust's reputation went beyond the borders of French-speaking countries. *Répression* came out in an English version as did its follow-up, *Marche ou Crève* (Savage, 1981). But Trust would refuse to go on a world tour with Judas Priest...

1980's *Répression*, Trust's second album, had the huge hit "Antisocial."

THE EIGHTIES: THE TRIUMPH OF HEAVY METAL
THE FIRST METAL MAIDENS

THEY APPEARED IN THE AFTERMATH OF THE PUNK REVOLUTION. THERE WEREN'T MANY OF THEM (STILL AREN'T), BUT THEY KNOCKED THE SOCKS OFF A UBER-MASCULINE SCENE.

JOAN JETT ("I LOVE ROCK'N'ROLL" 1981) AND LITA FORD ("OUT FOR BLOOD" 1983), BOTH FROM THE POP PUNK GROUP THE RUNAWAYS ("CHERRY BOMB" 1976).

One of the first all-female groups was

GIRL SCHOOL

fronted by a pair of singer-guitarists, Kim McAuliffe and Kelly Johnson (albums: *Demolition* and *Hit and Run*).

FANNY

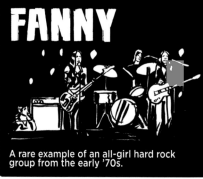

A rare example of an all-girl hard rock group from the early '70s.

THE PLASMATICS

The highly sexual Wendy O. Williams!

DORO PESCH

the German singer nicknamed "The Metal Queen" who founded the group Warlock in 1982, before going solo with Force Majeure in '89.

THE EIGHTIES: THE TRIUMPH OF HEAVY METAL
SPEED METAL

AS EARLY AS 1981, METAL WAS
BRANCHING OUT: SPEED, POWER,
GLAM, THRASH, BLACK, DEATH...

"SPEED" METAL, AS ITS
NAME INDICATES, IS HEAVY METAL
IN A HURRY. THE SPEED OF ITS
EXECUTION TURNS THE MUSICIAN
INTO AN ATHLETE. THE USE OF
DOUBLE PEDAL BASS DRUMMING
AND VERY RAPID RIFFS (SIXTEENTH
NOTES) PRODUCES AN ILLUSION
OF SPEED TWICE AS FAST AS
THE ACTUAL TEMPO.

TOP SPEED

pleasure to kill

"FAST AS SHARK" (ACCEPT, '82)
TOPPED OUT AT 140 BPM (BEATS PER
MINUTE) A YEAR BEFORE METALLICA'S
CLASSIC "KILL'EM ALL", KREATOR'S
"PLEASURE TO KILL", AND SLAYER'S
"REIGN IN BLOOD" UPPED IT TO
250 BPM IN 1986.

MODELS OF THE GENRE

The Canadians Anvil (*Metal on Metal*, '82)
and Exciter (*Heavy Metal Maniac*, '83).

THE EIGHTIES: THE TRIUMPH OF HEAVY METAL
POWER METAL

"POWER" METAL COMBINED THE VELOCITY OF SPEED METAL AND HEAVY METAL'S PENCHANT FOR MELODY, EMPHASIZING THE LATTER'S MOST GRANDILOQUENT FEATURES: MEDIEVAL SETTINGS, PIERCING VOCALS, THEATRICALITY. ITS U.S. ACTS FAVORED EPIC ATMOSPHERES DERIVED FROM HIGH FANTASY.

MANOWAR (*HAIL TO ENGLAND*, '84; *KINGS OF METAL*, '88; *THE TRIUMPH OF STEEL*, '92) SEEMED TO HAVE STEPPED STRAIGHT FROM THE VIRILE WORLD OF CONAN THE BARBARIAN. BASSIST JOEY DEMAIO, PYRO-TECH FOR BLACK SABBATH, AND GUITARIST ROSS "THE BOSS" (FROM THE FRENCH GROUP SHAKIN' STREET) SIGNED THEIR FIRST CONTRACT WITH THEIR OWN BLOOD! AND THOUGHT OF THEMSELVES AS GUARDIANS OF THE TEMPLE OF "TRUE METAL." THEY CLAIMED TO BE THE LOUDEST GROUP IN THE WORLD (RATIFIED BY THE GUINNESS BOOK OF WORLD RECORDS IN '84, AND AGAIN IN '92, TOPPING OUT AT 129 DECIBELS).

BALLS TO THE WALL

The genre experienced quite a boon in Germanic Europe with Accept, an elder statesman of the German scene along with Scorpions.

Their songs tackled realistic topics (lifestyles, inner conflicts, sexuality, discrimination) in a libertarian manner (albums: *Restless and Wild* in '82 and *Balls to the Wall* in '84).

Next, Helloween presided over the phantasmagorical stylings of the Quest and the Struggle between good and evil (*Walls of Jericho* in '86, *Keeper of the Seven Keys*, Parts I & II in '87 and '88).

THE EIGHTIES: THE TRIUMPH OF HEAVY METAL

GLAM

MTV METAL

MUSIC TELEVISION®

GLAM METAL WAS THE HOLLYWOOD HEIR TO ANDROGYNOUS BRITISH ROCK (SWEET) AND "SHOCK ROCK" (KISS) FROM THE '70S. ITS PRECURSOR:

DAVID LEE ROTH

THE EX-VAN HALEN VOCALIST AND CLOWNISH ACROBAT WHO COPIED THE VOCAL POSTURINGS OF FORMER GREATS ROBERT PLANT AND IAN GILLAN.

MY GOD!! THAT HAIR THOSE PINK GUITARS!!

Right from the start of the '80s, neurotic rockers reigned over L.A.'s Sunset strip, greedy for lust and luxury: Dokken, Poison, Ratt, Skid Row, Faster Pussycat.

CREW

FROM THE JUMBLE OF GLAM ROCK EMERGED A FEW RABBLE-ROUSING GROUPS LIKE MÖTLEY CRÜE (*SHOUT AT THE DEVIL*, '83; *GIRLS GIRLS GIRLS*, '87). THE NAME CAME FROM THE EXPRESSION A "MOTLEY CREW." IT WAS THE AMBITION OF THE ROWDY, UNRULY VINCE NEIL (VOCALS), NIKKI SIXX (BASS), TOMMY LEE (DRUMS) AND MICK MARS (GUITAR) TO BE THE MOST ORGIASTIC GROUP EVER: A GOAL SOON ATTAINED, AS THE 1991 COMPILATION DECADE OF DECADENCE ATTESTS.

People were lining up at labels' doors, which translated to millions in record sales—if MTV had featured it.

Hard FM was even more toned-down and radio-friendly (Foreigner, Journey, Bon Jovi)...

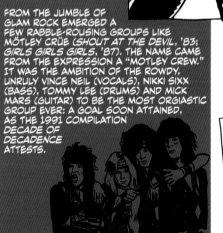

... and on the other side of the Atlantic, Europe with "The Final Countdown."

W.A.S.P.

SEXUAL PERVERTS

W.A.S.P. was the most outrageous, for their use of the acronym "White Anglo-Saxon Protestant" (singer Blackie Lawless claimed it stood for "We Are Sexual Perverts"), their hymn "Animal (Fuck Like a Beast)," and their onstage provocations (throwing meat at the public, simulating the torture of young women).

DEBAUCHERY

W.A.S.P. AND MÖTLEY CRÜE WERE THE FIRST BANES OF THE PMRC (PARENTS MUSIC RESOURCE CENTER), HEADED BY THE WIVES OF FAMOUS POLITICIANS (NANCY REAGAN, TIPPER GORE) WHO SAW ROCK AS AN INCITEMENT TO DEBAUCHERY, SUICIDE, AND SIMPLY PUT, SATANISM. WE HAVE THEM TO THANK FOR THE FAMOUS "PARENTAL ADVISORY" STICKER (WHICH WOULD HAVE THE EXACT OPPOSITE OF THE DESIRED EFFECT ON TEENS), LISTS OF SONGS AND GROUPS ("THE FILTHY FIFTEEN") TO BE BANNED FROM THE AIRWAVES—INCLUDING JUDAS PRIEST, AC/DC, BLACK SABBATH, ETC. AND EVEN A SENATE HEARING ON SEPTEMBER 19, 1985, FEATURING DEE SNIDER, TWISTED SISTER'S CLEAR-SIGHTED LEAD SINGER (NEW YORK, THE '84 HIT "I WANNA ROCK") WHO DECLARED:

PARENTAL ADVISORY EXPLICIT CONTENT

"PEOPLE WHO SEE PERVERSION EVERYWHERE — WHAT IS THEIR PROBLEM?"

UP TO ELEVEN

IN THE END, THE BEST DOCUMENTARY ABOUT GLAM METAL WAS *THIS IS SPINAL TAP* (1984), A FILM THAT JOYOUSLY MOCKED THE GENRE.

THE EIGHTIES: THE TRIUMPH OF HEAVY METAL
THRASH METAL

STARTING IN 1983, THRASH METAL (NOT TO BE CONFUSED WITH "TRASH ROCK") GAVE THE INSULAR LITTLE ANTHILL OF HEAVY METAL A GOOD HARD KICK.

THE POWER OF HEAVY METAL COMBINED WITH THE FURIOUS ENERGY OF HARDCORE PUNK (BLACK FLAG, MISFITS, SUICIDAL TENDENCIES): EVEN MORE AGGRESSIVE, UP-TEMPO, AND CLASHING COMPOSITIONS, SHOWCASING LOW TONES, SUDDEN RHYTHMIC BREAKS AND DISSONANCE IN THE **LOCRIAN MODE. IN E.** TILL THEN, HEAVY METAL HAD FAVORED THE AEOLIAN MODE (IN A).

RAGE

THRASH BROKE WITH THE FRIVOLOUSNESS OF GLAM METAL AND POWER METAL'S GRANDILOQUENT FANTASIES. IT EXPRESSED RAGE AND PESSIMISM IN THE FACE OF THE WORLD'S MADNESS: WAR, TYRANNY, SOCIAL VIOLENCE, CRIME, DRUGS...

FOUR GROUPS (WHOM CRITICS CALLED THE "BIG FOUR") STOOD OUT FROM THE THRASH HERD IN 1986: METALLICA (WITH THE ALBUM *MASTER OF PUPPETS*), MEGADETH (*PEACE SELLS... BUT WHO'S BUYING?*), ANTHRAX (*AMONG THE LIVING*), AND SLAYER (*REIGN IN BLOOD*). BUT THERE WERE OTHER NOTEWORTHY ACTS: TESTAMENT, OVERKILL, DEATH ANGEL...

DRESS CODE

Onstage presentation was never ostentatious: t-shirt and jeans, no flashy sets. The only thing that counted was the power of the performance, seen as an egalitarian group effort (bassists and drummers were as important as the classic lead singer-lead guitar duo).

MASTER OF PUPPETS

THE EIGHTIES: THRASH METAL
METALLICA

FOUNDED BY SINGER-GUITARIST JAMES HETFIELD AND DRUMMER LARS ULRICH, ALSO JOINED BY THE HIGHLY TALENTED KIRK HAMMETT (GUITAR) AND CLIFF BURTON (BASS), THE GROUP DEVELOPED QUICKLY, UNAFRAID TO ALIENATE HARDCORE PURISTS AND OLD-SCHOOL FANS.

KILL 'EM ALL

THEIR UNSTOPPABLE RISE BEGAN WITH *KILL 'EM ALL* ('83) AND *RIDE THE LIGHTNING* ('84). CLIFF BURTON'S UNFORTUNATE DEMISE IN A 1986 CAR ACCIDENT WHILE ON TOUR IN SCANDINAVIA DID NOT PUT A HALT TO THEIR ADVANCE.

THE ALBUMS *...AND JUSTICE FOR ALL* IN '88 AND *METALLICA* IN '91, WHICH CONTAINED SUCH CLASSICS AS "ENTER SANDMAN" AND "NOTHING ELSE MATTERS" EARNED METALLICA MASSIVE, UNPRECEDENTED WORLD-WIDE RECOGNITION NO METAL GROUP HAD ATTAINED SINCE LED ZEPPELIN.

LIVE SHIT: BINGE & PURGE

Metallica was the only metal group to headline major mainstream festivals, despite a marked creative decline and a controversial dispute with the free music downloading site Napster in the early aughts. Respectful of bands that had inspired its members in their youth, from Discharge to Motörhead, Metallica paid their influences a handsome tribute in their cover album *Garage Inc.*

THE EIGHTIES: THRASH METAL
MEGADETH

GROUP FOUNDED IN '83 BY GUITARIST **DAVE MUSTAINE**, AN ORIGINAL MEMBER OF **METALLICA** DISMISSED FROM THE GROUP EARLY ON. THIRSTING FOR REVENGE, HE TRIED (IN VAIN) TO ACHIEVE A SIMILAR LEVEL OF RECOGNITION. A FAN OF THE SEX PISTOLS, AND A SUBTLE, AGGRESSIVE MUSICIAN, OFTEN DAZZLING IF UNEVEN, MUSTAINE VIRULENTLY DENOUNCED THE HYPOCRISIES OF THE MILITARY-INDUSTRIAL COMPLEX.

RUST NEVER SLEEPS

MEGADEATH (WITH AN "A") IS A UNIT OF ONE MILLION CASUALTIES MEANT FOR ESTABLISHING HUMAN DEATH TOLLS DURING A GLOBAL NUCLEAR WAR.

MEGADETH REACHED THE PEAK OF ITS POPULARITY WITH THE ALBUMS *RUST IN PEACE* ('90) AND *COUNTDOWN TO EXTINCTION* ('92, FEAT. "SYMPHONY OF DESTRUCTION"). FRANCE FELL IN LOVE WITH THE BALLAD "À TOUT LE MONDE" ('94), WHOSE CHORUS WAS SUNG IN ACCENTED FRENCH.

MEGAPEACE

The video for "Peace Sells" ('86) has a clever self-referential moment when a father asks his son to turn on the news. The son, in a Slayer tee and deeply absorbed by a concert of Megadeth playing against a background of war footage, replies, "This is the news!"

THE EIGHTIES: THRASH METAL
ANTHRAX

ORIGINALLY FROM NYC, THE ONLY NON-CALIFORNIAN GROUP IN THE "BIG FOUR" (ANTHRAX/MEGADETH/METALLICA/SLAYER) AND THE ONLY ONE WITH A STRONG SENSE OF HUMOR. THEY CALL THEIR OWN MUSIC "MOSH" OR "POGO" METAL. THESE ODDBALLS IN BLACK JEANS, SKATERS AND COMIC GEEKS, LOVE BLENDING GENRES. ANTHRAX WOULD BE AMONG THE FIRST TO MERRILY MIX RAP AND METAL (THE EP *I'M THE MAN*, '87).

RICK ROLL

RICK RUBIN IS A GOOD EXAMPLE OF THE GROWING IMPORTANCE OF PRODUCERS IN THE LATE '80S. A VISIONARY MENTOR TO RUN-D.M.C. AND THE BEASTIE BOYS, HE IS ALSO A FAN OF METAL. HE PRODUCED MOST OF SLAYER'S ALBUMS, AS WELL AS ALBUMS BY DANZIG, RED HOT CHILI PEPPERS, THE CULT, SYSTEM OF A DOWN... AND LATE ALBUMS BY METALLICA (*DEATH MAGNETIC*, 2008) AND BLACK SABBATH (*13* IN 2013).

NOISE

Under the name S.O.D. (Stormtroopers of Death), some members of Anthrax offered up an avant-garde fusion of hardcore and heavy metal. We also owe Anthrax the English version of Trust's "Antisocial" from 1988!

And its version of Public Enemy's famous "Bring the Noise" in '91 would result in a daring duo tour. Racial harmony between audiences for rap and metal might seem counterintuitive at first. Rapper Chuck D said that it was one of his most difficult experiences ever. A few years earlier, Run-D.M.C. had covered Aerosmith's classic "Walk This Way"...

On the initiative of Rick Rubin, the founder of the label Def Jam.

THE EIGHTIES: THRASH METAL
SLAYER

MACABRE, GRIM... THERE'S NO SHORTAGE OF CUTTING ADJECTIVES TO DESCRIBE THE OEUVRE OF SLAYER, MADE UP OF TOM ARAYA (VOCALS AND BASS), KERRY KING, AND JEFF HANNEMAN (GUITAR), WHO DIED IN 2014.

DAVE LOMBARDO

IS THE DRUMMER WHOSE HARD-HITTING SPEED (UP TO 360 BPM) EARNED HIM THE NICKNAME "THE GODFATHER OF DOUBLEBASS."

LOMBARDO ALSO STOOD OUT FOR HIS EXPERIMENTAL SIDE PROJECTS: FANTÔMAS WITH MIKE PATTON AND ALBUMS WITH JOHN ZORN.

BUTCHER

"Angel of Death" ('86) featured the character of Joseph Mengele narrating his experiments on Jewish detainees at Auschwitz in the first person.

Morbid fascination, or a deliberate choice to narrate in a voice devoid of all moral judgment? The group denied the former and claimed the latter, but the question remains open.

In the violence of its lyrics, Slayer was a decisive influence on the Death and Black Metal scenes then just emerging.

GROUND ZERO

"JIHAD" FROM THE ALBUM ***CHRIST ILLUSION*** TACKLES MILITANT ISLAM FROM THE POV OF A CYNICAL WITNESS ("I WILL WATCH YOU DIE AGAIN FOR HIM") AND RELIGIOUS ZEALOT ("WHEN YOU REACH GROUND ZERO YOU WILL HAVE KILLED THE ENEMY/THE GREAT SATAN").

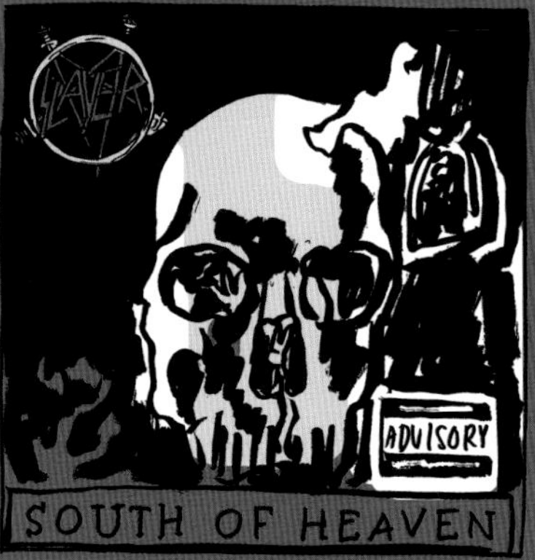
SLAYER
ADUISORY
SOUTH OF HEAVEN

ILLUSTRATOR LARRY CARROLL IS THE MAN BEHIND SEVERAL OF SLAYER'S MOST STRIKING ALBUM COVERS: *REIGN IN BLOOD*, *SOUTH OF HEAVEN*, *SEASONS IN THE ABYSS*, AND *CHRIST ILLUSION*.

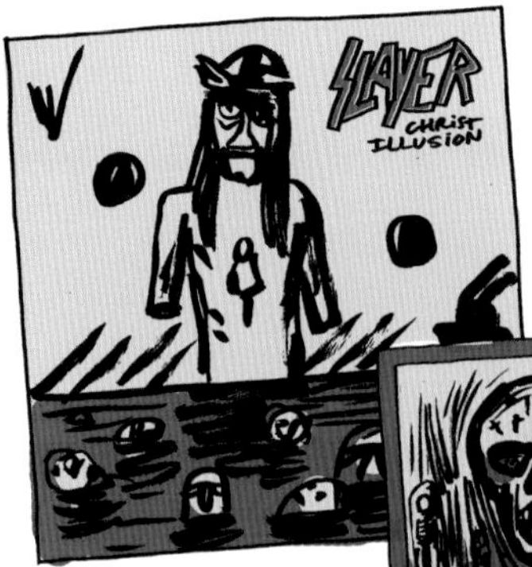
SLAYER
CHRIST ILLUSION

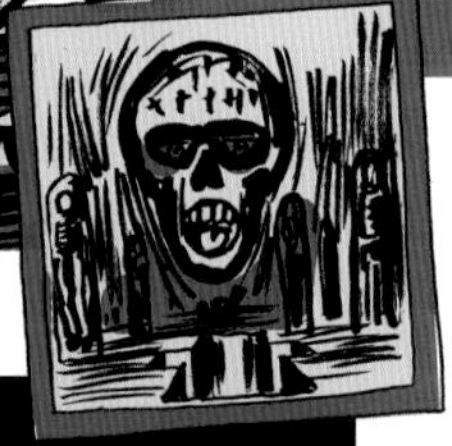

THE OTHER SCENE

for Thrash Metal was in Germany. Sodom, Destruction, and especially Kreator (the album *Pleasure to Kill*, '86) imposed an even harsher vision of the genre, a purism inspired by the Californians of Exodus (the album *Bonded by Blood*, '85), which had glam fans come onstage to be mocked with cries of "Kill the posers!"

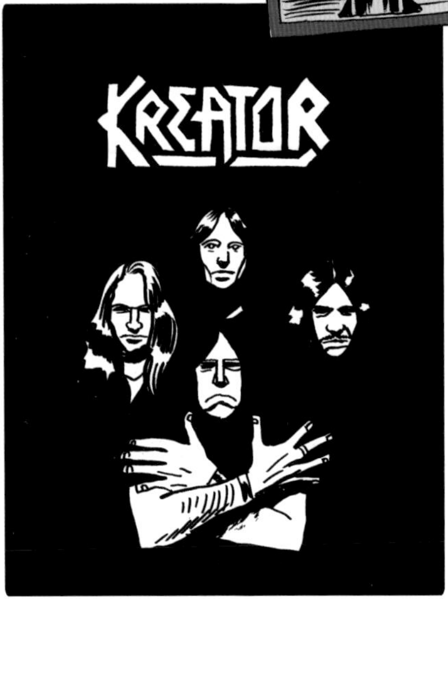
KREATOR

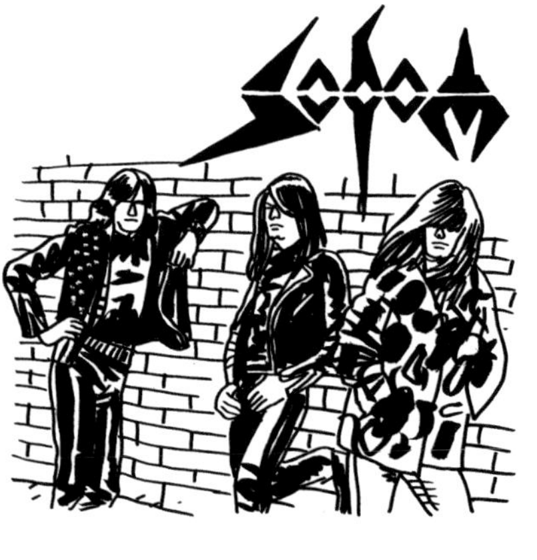
SODOM

THE BEGINNINGS OF EXTREME METAL
DEATH METAL

DEATH! DOOM! BLACK!

AS SOON AS ONE STYLE SEEMS TO FADE AWAY, OR GIVE IN TO THE SIREN SONG OF SELLING OUT, OTHER EVEN FIERCER STYLES BURST ONTO THE SCENE.

AS EARLY AS 1985, DEATH METAL DELIGHTED IN FEEDING ON THE MOST MORBID FORMS OF DEPRAVITY: MUTILATION, DISSECTION, NECROPHILIA...

ESCALATION

THE 1985 SONG "DEATH METAL" BY THE CALIFORNIAN GROUP POSSESSED (FROM THEIR ALBUM *SEVEN CHURCHES*) GAVE THE GENRE ITS NAME.

IT WAS A (IN)HARMONIOUS COMBINATION OF RADICAL TECHNOLOGICAL INNOVATION AND THE PERFECTION OF CERTAIN MUSICAL TECHNIQUES. VOCALS WERE MOURNFUL, GUTTURAL, OR ANGRY (THE "DEATH GROWL" THAT MADE LYRICS ALL BUT INDECIPHERABLE). LOGOS HAD TO BE ALMOST UNREADABLE. THE SOUND (LOWER TUNINGS AND MAX DISTORTION) WAS OMINOUS BUT CLEAR, THANKS TO "NOISE GATES" FILTERING SIGNAL FROM PARASITIC OSCILLATIONS. DRUMMING WAS SUPERFAST ("BLAST BEATS") WITH ABRUPT TEMPOS. THE CLASSIC VERSE/CHORUS STRUCTURE WAS BLOWN TO SMITHEREENS.

INVERTED CROSS

The first groups came from Tampa, Florida: Death (album: *Scream Bloody Gore*, '87) Morbid Angel (*Altars of Madness*, '89), Obituary, Deicide (whose lead singer had an inverted cross tattooed on his forehead!).

ESOTERISM

Death metal did not confine itself to a catalogue of horrors ripped from B-movie horror. Its penchant for death and suffering soon evolved toward more esoteric expressions. The genre was popularized by innovative labels (Metal Blade and its *Metal Massacre* compilations, Relapse, Earache).

The genre soon went international in the '90s: Poland (Vader), England (Carcass), Brazil (Overdose), and above all, Sweden (Entombed, Dismember, followed later by Meshuggah, In Flames, and At the Gates).

CANNIBAL

THE HIGHLY NECROPHILIAC BAND CANNIBAL CORPSE HAILED FROM BUFFALO. THEIR SONG TITLES SET THE TONE: "FUCKED WITH A KNIFE", "POST MORTAL EJACULATION".

RAAAARRGGH

DEATH METAL GAVE RISE TO SEVERAL VARIATIONS (FROM BRUTAL DEATH TO MELODIC DEATH) AND WAS CLOSE TO TWO EVEN FIERCER STYLES: METAL-CORE (THRASH METAL + PUNK HARDCORE) AND GRINDCORE (A PIERCING FUSION OF PUNK AND DEATH WHOSE PIONEERS WERE THE BRITISH PUNK ANARCHIST BAND NAPALM DEATH. THEIR '87 ALBUM *SCUM* FEATURED SUPER-SHORT SONGS: "YOU SUFFER" WAS BARELY OVER A SECOND LONG!

THE BEGINNINGS OF EXTREME METAL
DOOM METAL

DOOM METAL (FATE, RUIN, JUDGMENT, FAILURE, CALAMITY) IS THE MOST DIRECT DESCENDANT OF BLACK SABBATH AND LATE '60S HARD ROCK: SLOW TEMPOS, THICKER OR HEAVIER SOUNDS, MELANCHOLY ATMOSPHERE.

THE PIONEERS

PENTAGRAM AND SAINT VITUS. THE LATTER'S GUITARIST, SCOTT "WINO" WEINRICH, WAS INVOLVED IN SEVERAL GROUPS: THE OBSESSED, SPIRIT CARAVAN...

IN THE U.S.: PAGAN ALTAR, WITCHFINDER GENERAL. IN THE U.K.: CATHEDRAL. IN SWEDEN: CANDLEMASS (EPIC DOOM).

VOIVOD

THIS HIGHLY ORIGINAL QUEBECOIS GROUP FOUNDED IN '82 BY GUITARIST DENIS D'AMOUR AND SINGER DENIS BÉLANGER DREW ON SOPHISTICATED SCIENCE-FICTION VISUALS CREATED BY DRUMMER AND GRAPHIC DESIGNER MICHEL LANGEVIN. "VOIVOD" WAS A POST-APOCALYPTIC VAMPIRE LORD WHOSE APPEARANCE CHANGED WITH EVERY ALBUM.

CROWBAR

THE EARLY '90S

Doom would influence elegant British Gothic Metal (Paradise Lost, My Dying Bride, Anathema), and southwestern U.S. "Desert Rock" (Masters of Reality, Sleep, Kyuss), which was to become the source of late '90s Stoner Rock and harsh southern Sludge Metal (Crowbar).

MELVINS

THE BEGINNINGS OF EXTREME METAL
BLACK METAL

THIS VERY EUROPEAN COUSIN OF DEATH METAL STOOD OUT WITH ITS DISDAIN FOR TECHNICAL VIRTUOSITY, FAVORING INSTEAD PIERCING DISTORTED SOUNDS AND MAXIMUM REVERB.

LED BY BASSIST CRONOS, WHO LAUNCHED THE FAD FOR SCARY-SOUNDING STAGE NAMES (CRONOS WAS ZEUS' EVIL FATHER), THE BRITISH BAND VENOM WENT FOR BLASPHE-MOUS SATANIC IMAGERY ("WE DRINK THE VOMIT OF THE PRIESTS") AND HARSH SONIC CHAOS THAT OFFENDED CRITICS. BUT THE IMPACT OF SUCH ALBUMS AS *WELCOME TO HELL* ('81), *BLACK METAL* ('82), AND *AT WAR WITH SATAN* ('84)—THE STORY OF A WAR WHERE DEMONS DRIVE THE ANGELS FROM HEAVEN—WOULD PROVE LONG-LASTING.

WARRIOR

Also of note: the experimental Swiss band Celtic Frost, whose singer Tom Warrior was an ardent admirer of artist H.R. Giger and saw Black Metal as a catharsis for his violated childhood (the album *Into the Pandemonium*, '87); Bathory (Sweden), precursor of Viking Metal with its pagan connotations; and the profane scene in the Brazilian capital of metal Belo Horizonte, with bands like Holocausto and Sarcófago.

CONVERSION

DANISH KING DIAMOND WAS MORE SUBTLE, INSPIRED BY THE WRITINGS OF SATANIST ANTON LAVEY. FIRST WITH THE GROUP MERCYFUL FATE AND THEN UNDER HIS OWN NAME, HE OFFERED UP SOLEMNITY AND DECORUM WORTHY OF BLACK SABBATH.

The song "The Oath" ('84) tells the story of a Christian's conversion to Satanism, and has become the first classic of the genre.

Anton LaVey, who founded the Church of Satan in 1960s California, considered Satan the symbol of individual emancipation.

MADNESS ON THE BLACK METAL SCENE
NORWAY

A SECOND WAVE OF BLACK METAL DEVELOPED IN EARLY '90S NORWAY WITH MAYHEM, EMPEROR, BURZUM, AND DARKTHRONE. IT DREW UNFORTUNATE ATTENTION TO ITSELF ON POLICE BLOTTERS AND CRIME REPORTS.

IN OSLO, A BROTHERHOOD KNOWN AS THE "BLACK METAL INNER CIRCLE" FORMED AROUND MAYHEM'S DISTURBING GUITARIST EURONYMOUS. OUT OF IT GREW A RADICAL ANTI-CHRISTIAN IDEOLOGICAL MIXTURE: THE ERADICATION OF AN IMPORTED GOD AND A RETURN TO ANCESTRAL SPIRITUAL VALUES. THE EARLIEST SATANISM WAS REINTERPRETED AS "ODINISM".

VIOLENT WORDS GAVE WAY TO VIOLENT ACTS: THE BURNING OF ANCIENT RELIGIOUS EDIFICES (ON JUNE 6, 1992, AT 6 A.M. – "666" – THE WOODEN CHURCH IN FANTOFT BURST INTO FLAMES. IT WAS ACTUALLY CLOSER TO 4 A.M.)

NEXT CAME THE MURDER OF A GAY MAN BY THE DRUMMER OF EMPEROR, AND THEN THE DEATH OF EURONYMOUS–STABBED BY VARG VIKERNES, FOUNDER OF THE BAND BURZUM. ONCE HE HAD SERVED HIS JAIL SENTENCE, HE MOVED TO FRANCE.

EXTREMISM

Mayhem's lead singer, Dead, committed suicide with a shotgun in '92. Rumor has it that Euronymous, who found the body, made a necklace from the pieces of his skull before calling the police.

This extreme fringe of black metal still exists, especially present in the countries of the former Soviet Union, and claims affiliation with neo-Nazi ideas, but its audience is limited, and its ideas are rejected by the overwhelming majority of people in the genre (Tom Warrior calls them "primitive").

THE UNIVERSE EXPANDS

THE UNIVERSE OF BLACK METAL HAS GROWN BEYOND ITS PROTESTANT NORDIC ROOTS, SPREADING EVERYWHERE RELIGIOUS OPPRESSION MAKES ITSELF FELT: GREECE (ROTTING CHRIST), POLAND (BEHEMOTH), UKRAINE (DRUDKH, OR "WOOD" IN SANSKRIT), BELGIUM (ENTHRONED AND ANCIENT RITES), FRANCE (PESTE NOIRE OR "BLACK PLAGUE"), PORTUGAL (MOON-SPELL), EVEN DEEP IN MONOTHEISTIC LANDS (MELESCHESH, FROM JERUSALEM) AND THE MUSLIM WORLD (THE VERY UNDERGROUND AL-NAMR█████ OR "NIMROD" THE UNBELIEVE████ROM SAUDI ARABIA).

THROUGH THE REJECTION OF RELIGIOUS DOGMA, THIS INTROSPECTIVE MUSIC EVOKES, WITH GREAT INTENSITY, EXISTENTIAL QUESTIONS AND ENVIRONMENTALLY-MINDED PANTHEISTIC VISIONS (NACHTMYSTIUM, WOLVES IN THE THRONE ROOM).

A FEW GROUPS HAVE SUCCEEDED IN REACHING LARGER AUDIENCES (CRADLE OF FILTH, DIMMU BORGIR).

PAGAN METAL

Born of Black Metal, Pagan Metal refers to a subcultural cross-section encompassing various ancient heritages (Nordic, Celtic, Hellenic). Its livelier side, from the late '90s onward, was Folk Metal, which mixed metal with traditional instruments (bagpipes, mandolin, flute).

A proliferation that resulted in many branches: Celtic Metal, Medieval Metal, Oriental Metal... Skyclad (UK), Cruachan and Waylander (Ireland), In Extremo (Germany), Finntroll and Korpiklaani (Finland), Eluveitie (Switzerland), Arkona (Russia), Munruthel (Ukraine), Orphaned Land (Israel).

Is METAL TRULY SATANIC?

WHAT SANE PERSON COULD TRULY BELIEVE THAT ON THE 7TH DAY, WHEN GOD TOOK HIS REST, SATAN SEIZED THE CHANCE TO INVENT HEAVY METAL? SPEAKING SATAN'S NAME IS NO SUMMONS. ROCK AND BLUES HAVE MADE PLENTY USE OF THE DEVIL AS A FIGURE, BY TURNS A SUAVE SEDUCER (THE **ROLLING STONES'** "SYMPATHY FOR THE DEVIL", '68)...

AND A MALEFIC ENTITY (BLACK SABBATH AND **BLACK WIDOW** IN 1970, WITH THEIR SONG "COME TO THE SABBAT" FROM THE ALBUM *SACRIFICE*). THE LATTER CAUSED A STIR IN THE U.K. IN 1970 WITH THEIR HIGHLY REALISTIC STAGING OF THE BURNING OF A YOUNG VIRGIN.

CAPUCHIN FRIAR CESARE BONIZZI PLAYS IN THE GROUP FRATELLO METALLO ("BROTHER METAL").

HEAVY BIBLE

Satan also became a protest symbol. The figure of the Demon expressed a rejection of religious strictures, or else pagan and atheistic visions of existence.

Not all metalheads are heretics. Tom Araya (Slayer) and Dave Mustaine (Megadeth) are openly Catholic. There are dozens of "Christian metal" groups (the most famous being Stryper, which would pass out bibles after concerts in the late '80s), and some priests have even found Christian values in Heavy Metal!

CRUSADE

IN THE MID-'80S, AMERICAN RELIGIOUS FUNDAMENTALISTS LAUNCHED A CRUSADE AGAINST HEAVY METAL AS A "TOOL FOR THE PERVERSION OF YOUTH." NOT SATISFIED WITH SIMPLY TRYING TO FIND SUBLIMINAL SATANIC MESSAGES ON RECORDS OR DECIPHERING THE HIDDEN MEANING OF GROUP NAMES (EX. AC/DC = "AFTER CHRIST, DEVIL COMES" OR "ANTICHRIST / DEVIL'S CHILD"), THIS PARANOIA WOULD DEEM "THE DEVIL'S MUSIC" AN INCITEMENT TO CRIME.

☞ THE FILM "HELL'S BELLS: THE DANGERS OF ROCK'N'ROLL"

METAL TRIBUNAL

Fairly disturbing trials ensued, as if creators should be incriminated when their fans committed crimes. These proved in vain, as moralizing hysteria failed to sway judges.

In 1985, AC/DC was associated with serial killer Richard Ramirez, a fan of their song "Night Prowler".

JUDAS PRIEST

was accused in 1991 of causing the suicide—six years earlier, with their song "Stained Class"—of two teenagers abused by their alcoholic parents. The initiative came from lawyer Kenneth McKenna, who in '88 had already tried to implicate Ozzy Osbourne in a teenager's suicide for his song "Suicide Solution".

AND IN EUROPE...

EUROPE WAS NOT IMMUNE TO THESE TENDENCIES. AFTER THE ERFURT MASSACRE AT A GERMAN HIGH SCHOOL IN 2002, A RUMOR ACCUSED SLIPKNOT OF A SONG, "SCHOOL WARS," THAT DID NOT EXIST. IN FRANCE, MIVILUDES (THE INTERMINISTERIAL MISSION FOR MONITORING AND COMBATTING CULTIC DEVIANCES) NOTED IN 2004 THAT ATTENDANCE AT METAL CONCERTS IS NOT WITHOUT ITS RISKS: ALMOST HYPNOTIC ATMOSPHERES CONDUCIVE TO TRANCE STATES, SUBLIMINAL MESSAGES CALLING FOR ACTION AND STIMULATING SUICIDAL IMPULSES.

("SATANISM AND CULTIC DEVIANCE: THE RISKS AND HOW TO PREVENT THEM," 2004)

THE END OF THE '80S
METAL FOR EVERYONE

NONE OF THIS KEPT HEAVY METAL FROM REACHING UNPRECEDENTED HEIGHTS OF POPULARITY IN THE LATE '80S IN ITS MORE MAINSTREAM INCARNATIONS:

PROGRESSIVE METAL

HEIR TO '70S PROGRESSIVE ROCK: QUEENSRŸCHE, KING'S X, AND DREAM THEATER, ALL FEATURING SEASONED MULTI-INSTRUMENTALISTS.

QUEENSRŸCHE

TAKE HOLD OF THE FLAME

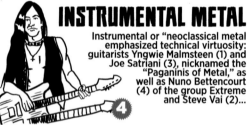

INSTRUMENTAL METAL

Instrumental or "neoclassical metal" emphasized technical virtuosity: guitarists Yngwie Malmsteen (1) and Joe Satriani (3), nicknamed the "Paganinis of Metal," as well as Nuno Bettencourt (4) of the group Extreme and Steve Vai (2)...

SCORPIONS

STILL LOVING YOU

AND THE FAMOUS ARPEGGIATED "POWER BALLAD": BUILT ON THE MODELS OF "DREAM ON" (AEROSMITH, '73) AND "LOVE HURTS" (NAZARETH, '75), IT SHOWED THAT HARD ROCKERS COULD BE BIG SOFTIES AT HEART. SCORPIONS SCORED WITH "STILL LOVING YOU" IN '84 AND AGAIN WITH "WIND OF CHANGE" IN '90, AND WHITESNAKE WITH "IS THIS LOVE" IN '87. ALL HEATING UP THE DANCE FLOOR...

POWER BALLAD

THE END OF THE '80S
GUNS N'ROSES

THE ULTIMATE INCARNATION OF AEROSMITH-STYLE HARD ROCK, BASED AROUND THE EXUBERANT SINGER, HOODLUM, AND CHARMER AXL ROSE (ADOPTED SON OF A PENTECOSTAL PREACHER), AND SLASH, A MIXED-RACE BRITISH GUITARIST. GUNS N'ROSES WILL GO DOWN IN THE BOOKS AS ONE OF THE BIGGEST COMMERCIAL SUCCESSES IN THE HISTORY OF MUSIC WITH ITS 1987 ALBUM *APPETITE FOR DESTRUCTION* (MORE THAN 25 MILLION COPIES SOLD) AND ITS TWO MEGA-HITS: THE BALLAD "SWEET CHILD O'MINE" AND THE HOSTILE "WELCOME TO THE JUNGLE," WHOSE VIDEO DEPICTS A YOUNG COUNTRY BOY ARRIVING IN THE CITY, DETERMINED TO BECOME A ROCK STAR.

GYPSY KINGS

THE BAND EMERGED FROM THE L.A. GLAM SCENE, BUT DID NOT GET LOST IN ITS SUPERFICIALITY. THEIR "GYPSY" STYLE (HINTED AT FIVE YEARS EARLIER BY THE FINNISH GROUP HANOI ROCKS) AND BRASH ARROGANCE MADE THE DIFFERENCE, EVEN WHEN THEIR MESSAGE WAS MUDDLED: THE SONG "ONE IN A MILLION" ('88) IS NARRATED BY A "SMALL TOWN WHITE BOY" JUST TRYING TO GET BY, WHO (FOR UNKNOWN REASONS) LASHES OUT AT THE POLICE, "NIGGERS," IMMIGRANTS, "FAGGOTS," RACISTS, AND LEFT-WING "RADICALS"...

DEMO CRACY?

But Rose's dictatorial and unpredictable nature made other members quit the group, despite the renewed success of albums like *Use Your Illusion* I & II in 1991. The most prolific career belonged to Slash (as a solo act and with the group Velvet Revolver, which had two other ex-Guns n' Roses members, Duff McKagan and Matt Sorum). It would take Axl Rose 10 years to cough up the pathetic *Chinese Democracy* (slated for '99, but not released till 2009).

THE END OF CLASSIC METAL
ALTERNATIVE METAL

THROUGHOUT THE '80S, FORMS OF UNDERGROUND ROCK THRIVED (NOISE, HARDCORE...) AND INVADED THE METAL SCENE IN THE EARLY '90S, RIDING THE GRUNGE WAVE (**NIRVANA**, MUDHONEY), GIVING BIRTH TO A PLETHORA OF "ALTERNATIVE" HYBRID FORMS.

NIRVANA

NIRVANA
NEVERMIND

RED HOT CHILI PEPPERS

SOUNDGARDEN

ALICE IN CHAINS
D I R T

Alice
In Chains,
Sound-
garden

1992

A constellation of innovative albums (in the wake of Nirvana's *Nevermind* and the Red Hot Chili Peppers' *Blood Sugar Sex Magik*, which came out the same day, September 24, 1991): Alice in Chains (*Dirt*), Body Count, Faith No More (*Angel Dust*), Helmet (*Meantime*), Kyuss (*Blues for the Red Sun*), Ministry (*Psalm 69*), Neurosis (*Souls at Zero*), Rage Against the Machine.

HARD CORE

Bio-hazard

HIP-HOP

see also the soundtrack to the films *Judgment Night* ('93) and *Spawn* ('97)

INDUSTRIAL ROCK

Ministry mixed digital sequences and sampled riffs. Nine Inch Nails was Trent Reznor's electro-metal project. Fear Factory...

GOTHIC ROCK + SYNTH

Type O Negative, White Zombie

STONER ROCK NEO-PSYCHEDELIA

Monster Magnet, Fu Manchu

FUNK ROCK

Faith No More, Red Hot Chili Pepers, Primus, Living Colour—one of the rare black rock groups with Fishbone and Bad Brain

NO METAL

BUT SOME OBJECTED TO ANY TIES WITH METAL: HELMET (WITH CUTTING, REPETITIVE MINIMALISM), THE DEFTONES (PRECURSOR OF NU METAL), AND THE INFLUENTIAL TOOL, WHICH DEVELOPED A KIND OF PROGRESSIVE ROCK ILLUSTRATED WITH SUMPTUOUS ESOTERIC VISUALS.

FACED WITH THIS BREAKING WAVE, CLASSIC HEAVY METAL WAS SOON SEEN AS OUTMODED. NOTABLE EXCEPTIONS INCLUDED METALLICA, AC/DC (WHO MADE A STUNNING COMEBACK WITH THE 1990 ALBUM *RAZOR'S EDGE* AND THE HIT "THUNDERSTRUCK"), AND OZZY OSBOURNE (WHO FOUNDED OZZFEST IN 1996). THE REST OF THE OLD GUARD MORE OR LESS RETIRED FROM THE SPOTLIGHT. "ALTERNATIVE METAL" WAS NOW THE BUZZWORD, AND A NEW GENERIC TERM "METAL" WAS ADOPTED. OZZFEST WELCOMED THIS NEW GENERATION, WHICH SAW HIM AS A GENUINE FATHER FIGURE.

THE END OF CLASSIC METAL
RAP METAL

RAP METAL COMBINES HIP HOP WITH HEAVY METAL.

IN 1992, RAGE AGAINST THE MACHINE OFFERED UP A FURIOUS COCKTAIL OF METAL, PUNK, AND RAP, WITH SUCH FIREBOMBS AS "BOMBTRACK" (A DIRECT CALL TO REBELLION), "KILLING IN THE NAME" (AND ITS EMBLEMATIC REFRAIN, "FUCK YOU, I WON'T DO WHAT YOU TELL ME!"), "BULLET IN THE HEAD" (AGAINST GULF WAR I), AND "KNOW YOUR ENEMY" ("CONFORMITY! SUBMISSION! HYPOCRISY! BRUTALITY! ALL OF WHICH ARE AMERICAN DREAMS!").

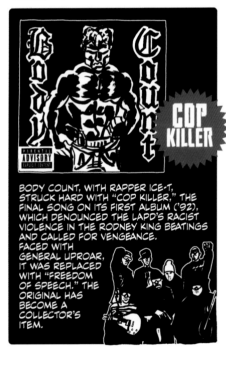

BODY COUNT, WITH RAPPER ICE-T, STRUCK HARD WITH "COP KILLER," THE FINAL SONG ON ITS FIRST ALBUM ('92), WHICH DENOUNCED THE LAPD'S RACIST VIOLENCE IN THE RODNEY KING BEATINGS AND CALLED FOR VENGEANCE. FACED WITH GENERAL UPROAR, IT WAS REPLACED WITH "FREEDOM OF SPEECH." THE ORIGINAL HAS BECOME A COLLECTOR'S ITEM.

rage against the machine

RAGE INSIDE

Next came the albums *Evil Empire* ('96) and *The Battle of Los Angeles* ('99), for which Michael Moore directed the videos.

Singer Zack de la Rocha then left the band. The three other members of RATM founded Audioslave in 2001 on the initiative of guitarist Tom Morello, with Soundgarden singer Chris Cornell. Audioslave was the first U.S. rock group to play Cuba (a concert in Havana on May 6, 2005).

THE END OF CLASSIC METAL
GROOVE METAL

GROOVE METAL IS AN OFFSPRING OF THRASH METAL TINGED WITH SCATHING, SYNCOPATED RIFFS: PRONG, MACHINE HEAD, AND ABOVE ALL, PANTERA (FROM TEXAS) AND SEPULTURA (BRAZIL) ARE ITS LEADERS. AFTER YEARS OF WAVERING BETWEEN GLAM AND POWER METAL, PANTERA UPPED THE ANTE WITH 1990'S *COWBOYS FROM HELL*. SCREAMING "YOU'RE MAKING US FUCKING HOSTILE" (FROM THE 1992 ALBUM *VULGAR DISPLAY OF POWER*), THEY BECAME THE SPOKESMEN FOR A GENERATION NO LONGER SATISFIED WITH MOURNFUL GRUNGE.

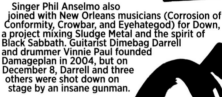

Singer Phil Anselmo also joined with New Orleans musicians (Corrosion of Conformity, Crowbar, and Eyehategod) for Down, a project mixing Sludge Metal and the spirit of Black Sabbath. Guitarist Dimebag Darrell and drummer Vinnie Paul founded Damageplan in 2004, but on December 8, Darrell and three others were shot down on stage by an insane gunman.

Phil Anselmo's tats photo by Pulitzer-winner John Kaplan.

MONSTER RUSSIA

THE RUSSIAN EDITION OF THE MONSTERS OF ROCK FESTIVAL ON SEPTEMBER 28, 1991—WITH PANTERA, AC/DC, AND METALLICA—GATHERED ALMOST A MILLION PEOPLE AT AN AIRPORT ON MOSCOW'S OUTSKIRTS AGAINST A BACKDROP OF HIGH POLITICAL TENSION. CONFRONTATIONS BETWEEN ATTENDEES AND SOLDIERS TASKED WITH KEEPING ORDER RESULTED IN SEVERAL DEATHS.

TI E END OF CLASSIC METAL
SEPULTURA

SEPULTURA WAS FOUNDED BY BROTHERS MAX AND IGOR CAVALERA IN BELO HORIZONTE, THE BRAZILIAN CAPITAL OF METAL EVER SINCE THE EARLY '80S. (MAX SAID THE CITY "HAD MORE CHURCHES THAN CLEAN HOUSES"). FROM 1985 ONWARD, THE BAND OFFERED A FURIOUS FUSION OF THRASH AND DEATH METAL, POLITICALLY ENGAGED DESPITE IRON MILITARY RULE.

MAX THE MENACE

AFTER LEAVING THE GROUP, MAX CAVALERA FOUNDED SOULFLY IN 1998. TEN YEARS LATER, HE REUNITED WITH HIS BROTHER FOR CAVALERA CONSPIRACY.

AMONG HIS SIDE PROJECTS WAS THE EXPERIMENT NAILBOMB, AN AVANT-GARDE MIXTURE OF THRASH AND INDUSTRIAL METAL WITH ENGLISHMAN ALEX NEWPORT OF FUDGE TUNNEL. IT LASTED FOR ONLY ONE ALBUM IN '94 AND A CONCERT THE NEXT YEAR (IN HOLLAND, AT DYNAMO OPEN AIR).

BLOODY ROOTS

Sepultura experienced the beginnings of international fame in '88 after Max went to New York to land a contract. The group put together just enough for a one-way flight. Success soon followed with the albums *Chaos A.D.* (1993)—featuring the anti-authority hymn "Refuse/Resist"—and *Roots* (1996), chock full of wild Afro-Brazilian percussion and tribal Amazonian rhythms.

THE END OF CLASSIC METAL
NU-METAL

NU METAL, A FUSION OF ALL THESE ELEMENTS IN THE SECOND HALF OF THE '90S, INNOVATED IN TERMS OF INSTRUMENTATION: DIGITAL EFFECTS, SEVEN-STRING GUITARS (THE FAMOUS IBANEZ UNIVERSE), AND FIVE- OR SIX-STRING BASSES, WHICH TILL THEN HAD BEEN THE PROVINCE OF CERTAIN VIRTUOSOS. THE TURN OF THE CENTURY SAW RECOGNITION FOR **KORN** (WITH THEIR 1998 ALBUM *FOLLOW THE LEADER*), **SLIPKNOT** (*SLIPKNOT* IN '99 AND *IOWA* IN '01), AND **SYSTEM OF A DOWN** (*TOXICITY* IN '01).

The first herald of the genre with the 1994 single "Blind" and the 1996 album *Life Is Peachy*: Jonathan Davis' screams and growls gave off a deep sense of unease (like a Robert Smith of metal).

ROSS PRODUCTION

ROSS ROBINSON COACHED KORN AND SLIPKNOT. HE ALSO PRODUCED LIMP BIZKIT, MACHINE HEAD, AND SEPULTURA.

SLIPKNOT HAILED FROM THE MIDWEST (DES MOINES, IOWA) AND WAS INFLUENCED BY NEW WAVE HORROR MOVIES (*SCREAM*, *SAW*). ITS NINE MASKED MEMBERS WERE IDENTIFIED BY NUMBERS AND NICKNAMES. FOUNDER AND DRUMMER SHAWN CRAHAN, KNOWN AS "CLOWN," WAS #6. CONCERTS FORMED A NIHILISTIC WHIRL CULMINATING WHEN THE CROWD TOOK UP THE CRY "PEOPLE = SHIT".

SYSTEM
OF A DOWN

Founded by members of the Armenian diaspora (singer Serj Tankian and guitarist Daron Malakian), SOAD was without a doubt the most unclassifiable group on the new American scene.

SYSTEM OF A DOWN

Highly eclectic in their influences (they mixed clashing metal, Zappa-esque collages, and elements of their native musical culture), and very political (ex. the anti-Iraq-war song "B.Y.O.B." – Bring Your Own Bombs), the band managed to win over a large non-metal (and very female) audience in Europe with their albums *Mezmerize* and *Hypnotize*.

In 2015, System of a Down took part in commemorating the centennial of the Armenian genocide (the Wake Up the Souls Tour), playing for the first time in Erevan, Armenia.

SHOW BIZ

A MORE COMMERCIAL KIND OF NU METAL TRIUMPHED WITH LIMP BIZKIT (WHOSE LEAD SINGER, FRED DURST, NAVIGATED FASHIONABLE HIP-HOP TRENDS WITH EASE), LINKIN PARK, PAPA ROACH, AND GODSMACK.

MONSTERS
OF ROCK

MONSTER DISGUISES HAVE LONG BEEN A PART OF THE CULTURE OF HEAVY METAL. "SCREAM METAL" STARTED IN 1985 WITH THE SATIRICAL BAND GWAR, WHOSE COSTUMES WERE INSPIRED BY LOW-BUDGET SCIENCE-FICTION AND HORROR. THE FINNISH BAND LORDI FOLLOWED SUIT, AND WENT ON TO WIN THE EUROVISION CONTEST IN 2006.

ROB ZOMBIE

THIS BRAND OF SCARE OR HORROR METAL ALSO BROUGHT FORTH ROB ZOMBIE, WHO IN ADDITION TO HIS MUSICAL CAREER HAS DIRECTED SIX MOVIES SINCE *HOUSE OF 1000 CORPSES* IN 2003.

10 YEARS OF UPHEAVAL
1990S

1990-1999: TEN YEARS OF TURNING EVERYTHING UPSIDE DOWN, FROM LOOKS (GOATEES, PIERCINGS, SLASHED-UP SPORTSWEAR) TO MEANS OF MUSICAL DISTRIBUTION (SOUNDTRACKS FOR SKATEBOARDING VIDEOS, ADS FOR CLOTHES, AND MOVIES LIKE *THE CROW*, *SPAWN*, ETC.). TEN YEARS OF SONGS THAT SPOKE CATHARTICALLY ABOUT THE LOSS OF BEARINGS AND PERSPECTIVES, AND OFTEN, CHILDHOOD ABUSE (EX. TOOL'S "PRISON SEX" AND KORN'S "HEY DADDY"). A MALAISE THAT SOMETIMES LED TO A RETURN TO RELIGION (TWO OF KORN'S MUSICIANS BECAME BORN-AGAIN CHRISTIANS)!

THE CROW

ANTICHRIST

An androgynous cross-dresser would prove the best symbol for this chaos: Brian Warner, a.k.a. Marilyn Manson (hitching together two strong symbols of death in America: the iconic actress and the serial killer). This protégé of Trent Reznor, an expert at disturbing covers of pop hits (the Eurythmics' "Sweet Dreams") proved a master at subverting puritan ideas

WHITE TRASH

THE SCABROUS "CAKE AND SODOMY" ("WHITE TRASH GET DOWN ON YOUR KNEES TIME FOR CAKE AND SODOMY") IN 1994 AND THE PROVOCATIVE "ANTI-CHRIST SUPERSTAR" IN '96 EARNED MANSON LONG-LASTING HATRED. HE WAS EVEN ACCUSED OF INSPIRING THE 1999 COLUMBINE SHOOTINGS.

On April 20, 2 boys at a Colorado high school killed 12 of their fellow students.

11:57:20-63 AM

(which he knew well: see his auto-biography, *The Long Hard Road Out of Hell*). The title of the French version, *Memoirs of Hell*, almost gives the wrong impression—that he enjoyed it.

HELL ON CELLOS

THE LATE '90S WITNESSED A FE
UNUSUAL ARTIFACTS EMERGING FRO
EUROPE: APOCALYPTICA (FINLAN
TACKLED METAL WITH CELLOS. THE
FIRST ALBUM, IN '96, CONSISTE
ENTIRELY OF METALLICA COVER

RAMMSTEIN

Rammstein, which came out
of the East Berlin punk scene,
sang highly warlike Industrial
Metal in German, carried by
spectacular porno-pyrotechnic
stagecraft.

Their first album, *Herzeleid*
("heartbreak") in '95 drew the
attention of David Lynch, who
used two songs from it in his
movie *Lost Highway*.

DESPITE ACCUSATIONS OF PAN-GERMANIC
NATIONALISM, THE BAND ACHIEVED INTERNATIONAL
RECOGNITION WITH THEIR ALBUMS *SEHNSUCHT*
('97), *MUTTER* (2001), AND THE CAUSTIC HIT
"AMERIKA" ('04). THE "AMERIKA" OF "COCA-COLA"
WAS "WUNDERBAR" BUT ALSO "SOMETIMES WAR."

THE 21ST CENTURY BEGINS:
MOSAIC

INNOVATIVE COLLECTIVES OFFERED UNPRECEDENTED MASHUPS. THERE WAS THE PROGRESSIVE DARK METAL OF MASTODON, HEIR TO NEUROSIS AND TOOL (SIX ALBUMS, INCLUDING 2006'S *BLOOD MOUNTAIN*). THE METALCORE OF CONVERGE (EIGHT ALBUMS INCLUDING THE ABRUPT *NO HEROES* IN 2006), WHOSE GUITARIST, KURT BALLOU, RALLIED SEVERAL OTHER TALENTED GROUPS (CAVE IN, TORCH) TO HIS LABEL DEATHWISH AND HIS STUDIO GODCITY. AND THE JAZZ METAL OF NORWEGIAN GROUP SHINING (SEVEN ALBUMS, INCLUDING 2010'S *BLACK JAZZ*).

THE NEW WAVE OF AMERICAN HEAVY METAL

MIXED GUTTURAL AND MELODIOUS EFFECTS: AVENGED SEVENFOLD, KILLSWITCH ENGAGE, LAMB OF GOD...

IN QUEBEC
ABRASIVE PRESENCES BURST ONTO THE SCENE–KATAKLYSM, CRYPTOSY, DESPISED ICON–SHAKING UP THE THRASH METAL TRADITION AND BACKED BY THE LABEL GALY.

RETRO

But Metal was also entering a slightly retro recycling phase, marked by the return of Nordic, epic Power/Death Metal (Hammerfall, Sabaton, Children of Bodom) and the success of pompous "Symphonic Metal": Nightwish and Stratovarius (Finland), Therion (Sweden), Lacuna Coil and Rhapsody of Fire (Italy), Angra (Brazil), Within Temptation, Epica, After Forever (The Netherlands).

METAL(E)

A handful of women singers flipped the bird at macho clichés: Tairrie B (My Ruin), Candace (Walls of Jericho), Otep, and the group Kittie...

DRONE

A METAL COUSIN OF POST-ROCK, DRONE MUSIC VENTURED INTO HYPNOTIC SOUNDSCAPES BASED ON A SINGLE NOTE OR SUSTAINED TONE-CLUSTER (THE "DRONE"), FULL OF REVERB AND SUB-BASS. GROUPS INCLUDE EARTH, ISIS, AND SUNN O IN THE U.S., CULT OF LUNA IN SWEDEN, AND BORIS IN JAPAN...

TH 21ST CENTURY BEGINS:
THE APOGEE OF STONER ROCK

KYUSS/QOTSA

BETWEEN HEAVY, DOOM-LADEN RHYTHMS AND THE HALLUCINATORY SOUNDS OF OLD PSYCHEDELIC ROCK, STONER ROCK UNDERWENT A SUDDEN EXPANSION IN THE WAKE OF KYUSS. ITS LIFE AS A BAND WAS SHORT (1990-96), BUT ITS EFFECT MASSIVE, WITH THE ALBUMS *BLUES FOR THE RED SUN* ('92) AND *WELCOME TO SKY VALLEY* ('94). ITS INFLUENTIAL MUSICIANS INCLUDED BRANT BJORK, JOHN GARCIA, NICK OLIVERI, AND JOSH HOMME, WHO LAUNCHED THE DESERT SESSIONS. FROM THE CRADLE OF KYUSS EMERGED QUEENS OF THE STONE AGE, MONDO GENERATOR, HERMANO, VISTA CHINO...

IN 2004, DAVE GROHL, NIRVANA DRUMMER AND LEADER OF THE NEO-GRUNGE BAND FOO FIGHTERS, PAID TRIBUTE TO THE METAL SINGERS OF HIS TEENAGE YEARS WITH THE ASTONISHING ALBUM *PROBOT*, WHICH GATHERED TWELVE LEGENDS FROM THE '80S AND '90S: CRONOS, LEMMY, TOM WARRIOR, MAX CAVALERA, ETC. HE OFFERED EACH GUEST A SONG TO WRITE LYRICS TO AND SING. IN 2009, GROHL TOOK PART IN THE SHORT-LIVED THEM CROOKED VULTURES WITH JOSH HOMME (QUEENS OF THE STONE AGE) AND JOHN PAUL JONES (OF LED ZEPPELIN!).

Like other old-timers who were still active (Monster Magnet), they were guides to a prolific brood worldwide: Burning Witch, Orange Goblin, Spiritual Beggars, Nebula, Electric Wizard, and more recently, Red Fang, Witchcraft, Kadavar, Uncle Acid... backed by such specialized labels as Rise Above, Man's Ruin, Southern Lord...

OLD SCHOOL HARD

Stoner brought about a late renaissance of "Old School" hard rock led by The Darkness

(UK), The Answ (Ireland), and Australians Wo Mother (a veritable Zeppelin clone) and Airbourne (whose work sounded inspire by the ghost of Bon Scott).

FRANCE: THE SCENE BLOWS UP
THE 1990-2000 DECADE

PIONEERS OF MODERN METAL IN THE LATE '80S, THE YOUNG GODS (SWITZERLAND) AND **TREPONEM PAL** (PARIS, '89), BARDS OF INDUSTRIAL METAL, WERE FOLLOWED BY **LOFOFORA** ('94), WHOSE REBELLIOUS FUSION METAL DREW IMITATORS (MASS HYSTERIA, WATCHA, MASNADA) AND FRENCH NU METAL: ENHANCER, PLEYMO, AQME, ETHS (FROM MARSEILLE, WITH REMARKABLE PAIN-RIDDEN LYRICS BY SINGER CANDICE).

FRENCH PARADOX

A lively Death Metal scene developed from 2000 onwards: Gojira (Bayonne), Gorod (Bordeaux), Dagoba (Marseille), Trepalium and Hacride (Poitiers), Scarve (Nancy)... Black Metal was also around: Anorexia Nervosa (Limoges), Peste noire (Avignon)...

METAL HURLANT

BUT CHANCES TO MAKE A NAME BEYOND FRENCH BORDERS REMAINED SCARCE. THE SCENE DIDN'T REALLY SPREAD. ONLY GOJIRA, UNDER THE LEADERSHIP OF THE DUPLANTIER BROTHERS, SUCCEEDED.

THEIR PROGRESSIVE DEATH METAL EMANATED SUCH SPIRITUAL INTENSITY THAT IT LED THEM TO HEIGHTS NO OTHER FRENCH GROUP HAD EVER REACHED. THEIR THIRD ALBUM, 2005'S *FROM MARS TO SIRIUS*, WAS PICKED UP FOR DISTRIBUTION OVERSEAS AND MARKED THE DEBUT OF A PROMISING INTERNATIONAL BREAKTHROUGH THAT FOUND CONFIRMATION IN 2008 DURING AN AMERICAN TOUR WITH METALLICA. EVER SINCE THEN, THE GROUP'S FAME HAS ONLY CONTINUED TO GROW WITH SUCH ALBUMS AS *THE WAY OF ALL FLESH* AND *L'ENFANT SAUVAGE*.

EXTREME EXTREME

Extreme Switzerland: Samael, Nostromo, Rorcal, Mumakil, Kruger... Extreme Belgium: Amen Ra, Aborted, Length of Time...

LABELS

GOJIRA SIGNED IN ITS EARLY DAYS WITH EXTREME METAL LABEL LISTENABLE, ACTIVE SINCE 1990 AND BASED IN PAS-DE-CALAIS, A REGION ALSO HOME TO THE LABEL OSMOSE, FOUNDED IN 1991. ALSO WORTHY OF MENTION IS SEASON OF MIST, FOUNDED IN MARSEILLE IN 1996

WORLD METAL

NOTHING HALTED THE SPREAD OF METAL WORLDWIDE BEYOND ITS ENGLISH-SPEAKING ORIGINS AND ITS FIRST INROADS: GERMAN AND SCANDINAVIAN EUROPE, AND THEN IN THE '80S, SOUTHERN EUROPE, BRAZIL, JAPAN. TODAY, THE SPREAD OF METAL HAS REACHED THE SLAVIC COUNTRIES, THE MUSLIM WORLD, AND THE FAR EAST. AFRICA REMAINS AN EXCEPTION, BUT RECENTLY METAL HAS BEEN REPORTED IN KENYA AND ANGOLA.

A WHIFF OF SULFUR

At first, Metal was exported in commercialized Western forms. But original scenes combining characteristics of Heavy Metal and traditional sounds soon developed all over.

These struggle to exist in often difficult, even dangerous political conditions: Metal is often still seen as having a whiff of Satanic sulfur to it, leading to accusations of apostasy* (in Jordan and Malaysia). Sometimes it is indulged in almost total secrecy. The Iranian film *No One Knows About Persian Cats* (which won a prize at Cannes in 2009) bears witness to how hard metal artists' daily lives are in the face of the regime's hardline dogma.

In Morocco in 2003, 14 fans and musicians (from the group Infected Brain and Nekros) were sentenced to prison by a Casablanca court—a verdict soon reversed after protests.

ROCKUMENTARIES

SEE ALSO THE DOCUMENTARIES *GLOBAL METAL* (SAM DUNN, 2008), *DEATH METAL ANGOLA* (JEREMY XYDO, 2012), AND *UN MONDE DE METAL* (*A WORLD OF METAL*, OLIVIER RICHARD, 2015)

* apostasy: public renunciation of faith

MELECHESH,

a group of Assyrian and Armenian origin founded in 1993, based in Jerusalem and Bethlehem. Its music invokes old Mesopotamian myths. In 1999, the band moved to the Netherlands, officially for personal reasons (pursuing higher education). But in reality, they were tired of the nonstop pressure from Orthodox fundamentalists.

HEAVY MUSLIM

A FEW NAMES FROM AMONG HUNDREDS OF GROUPS ACTIVE IN THE MUSLIM WORLD: ZIGGURAT AND MEZARKABUL IN TURKEY...

TOTAL ECLIPSE IN MOROCCO, LITHAM AND LELAHELL IN ALGERIA, ARSAMES AND MASTER OF PERSIA IN IRAN, JAMRUD AND VALLENDUSK IN INDONESIA, THE FEMALE GROUP **MASSIVE SCAR ERA** IN EGYPT...

INSTRUMENT OF TORTURE

A STRANGE ERA THAT ALSO SAW THE U.S. ARMY USE HEAVY METAL FOR PSYCHOLOGICAL TORTURE IN THE SECRECY OF GUANTANAMO BAY (BLASTING IT AT TOP VOLUME INTO CELLS FOR HOURS), DESPITE PROTESTS FROM METALLICA ("ENTER SANDMAN" WAS A FAVORITE OF JAILERS) AND OTHER GROUPS. AND SO, IN 2014, THE CANADIAN GROUP SKINNY PUPPY INVOICED THE PENTAGON FOR $666,000 FOR ILLEGALLY DOWN-LOADING THEIR MUSIC AND USING IT FOR IMMORAL PURPOSES.

BILOCATE IN JORDAN, MYRATH IN TUNISIA, **BETZEFER** AND ARALLU IN ISRAEL, THE FRANCO-MAGHREBI GROUP ARKAN, FOUNDED IN 2005 BY FOUED MOUKID...

BACK IN BLACK...
TO THE FUTURE!

2015: THE NEAR FUTURE OF HEAVY METAL IS STILL BEING FORGED, IN THE SHADOW OF MYTHIC NAMES FROM THE PAST NOW BACK IN THE SPOTLIGHT AFTER BEING FORGOTTEN IN THE '90S: A LONG, CONSERVATIVE WAVE THAT IS KEEPING THEIR HEIRS FROM RISING. AFTER THE ORIGINAL BLACK SABBATH'S BRIEF REUNION IN 1997, THERE WAS A PASSING FAD OF BANDS GETTING BACK TOGETHER: BRUCE DICKINSON AND IRON MAIDEN IN 1999, ROB HALFORD AND JUDAS PRIEST FIVE YEARS LATER.

666

In 2008, Iron Maiden was able to measure its popularity during a world tour with a Boeing 757 customized a "Flight 666" and piloted by the lead singer. AC/DC (which lost founding member Malcolm Young in 2015) and KISS have been active for 40 years as of 2013, and Motörhead as of 2015. And elder statesmen Judas Priest and Scorpions (45-year careers as of 2014) extended their farewell tours in response to an ecstatic reception.

Ever since, big names from the past have begun headlining again, and even "obscure" groups like Anvil (see the 2008 film *The Story of Anvil*) were given a new chance.

THE COME BLACK

AT LONG LAST, AFTER THE HEAVEN & HELL INTERLUDE (*THE DIO YEARS*, 2006-10), BLACK SABBATH RE-ENTERED THE SCENE WITH *13* IN 2013, 45 YEARS AFTER STARTING OUT. THE FIRST STUDIO ALBUM WITH OZZY OSBOURNE SINCE '78, IT ASKED "GOD IS DEAD?" FOR THE GODS OF METAL, THE QUESTION IS MORE LIKE: HOW MUCH LONGER? FOR THEY ARE, IN THE END, MORTAL. HEAVY METAL WILL MOURN THEIR PASSING, BUT ITS VIBRANT CULTURE WILL GO ON...

SUGGESTIONS FOR FURTHER READING

THREE RECOMMENDATIONS FROM JACQUES DE PIERPONT

Sound of the Beast: The Complete Headbanging History of Heavy Metal, by Ian Christe (Allison & Busby cop., 2004). Dense, detailed, and rich in juicy anecdotes, a very American vision of Heavy Metal that partakes wholeheartedly in the excesses of its subject with its lyricism ("Heavy Metal remains mysterious and very much alive, a search for truth in a storm of folly.") and passionate subjectivity (Metallica and Black Sabbath form the book's through-line).

Anthropologie du metal extrême [Anthropology of Extreme Metal], by Nicolas Walzer (Camion blanc, 2007). Sociologist and fan, Walzer devoted his doctoral thesis at the Sorbonne to a well-researched exploration of the philosophy of life that goes with the radical aesthetics of Black Metal. Drawing on long interviews with dozens of people from the French scene, he pushes past cliché toward a Promethean imagery rich in "symbolique sacrality."

Une histoire musicale du rock [A Musical History of Rock], by Christophe Pirenne (Fayard, 2011). A valuable guide and would-be encyclopedia that examines the history of rock (in the broadest sense, of "amplified music") through an (initially, but not solely) musical lens. "Metalheads" get their day in the sun, set carefully in a larger context. Specialized but never abstruse, though a minimum of musical knowledge will make it easier.

SUGGESTIONS FOR FURTHER READING

THREE RECOMMENDATIONS FROM HERVÉ BOURHIS

White Line Fever: The Autobiography, by Lemmy Kilmister and Janiss Garza (Simon & Schuster UK Ltd., 2016). Otherwise known as the memoirs of Motörhead's lead singer. Music, religion, sex, drugs, high times, twists of fate, stormy relationships with the recording industry put through the mill of a clear and caustic mind. The title is taken from a song about speed, "It's a slow death... It hasn't killed me yet."

The Art of Metal: Five Decades of Heavy Metal Album Covers, Posters, T-Shirts and More, by Martin Popoff and Malcolm Dome (London Omnibus Press, 2013). In Metal, image and music enter into close symbiosis. This deep dive into a rich visual world across multiple media (record sleeves, posters, logos, t-shirts) shines a spotlight on many artists—painters, photographers, and illustrators: Drew Struzan, Hugh Syme, Rosław Szaybo, Dave Patchett... (the only shortcoming: the absence of "fantasy" themed work linked to Power Metal, from Dio to Manowar).

Anvil: The Story of Anvil, dir. Sacha Gervasi, 2008. Metal. Destiny. Friendship. Bad luck. Redemption. Will make you cry from sadness and awesomeness.

THE LITTLE BOOK OF KNOWLEDGE

JÉRÔME
PIERRAT

TATTOOS

ALFRED

THE LITTLE BOOK OF KNOWLEDGE

JACQUES

HEAVY METAL

HERVÉ

BERNARD
SÉRET

SHARKS

JULIEN
SOLÉ

THE LITTLE BOOK OF KNOWLEDGE

JEAN-BAPTISTE
THORET

**NEW
HOLLYWOOD**

BRÜNO

THE LITTLE BOOK OF KNOWLEDGE

THE LITTLE BOOK
OF KNOWLEDGE:

HEAVY METAL